New York

LOOK BOOK

Published by

 MELCHER MEDIA

124 West 13th Street
New York, NY 10011
www.melcher.com

Distributed in the U.S.
by DK Publishing
www.dk.com

Publisher: Charles Melcher
Associate Publisher: Bonnie Eldon
Editor in Chief: Duncan Bock
Editor: Holly Rothman
Assistant Editor: Shoshana Thaler
Production Director: Kurt Andrews

Design by Circle & Square

© 2007 New York Magazine Holdings LLC

Text and Interviews by Amy Larocca
All photographs © 2007 Jake Chessum
except pages 4, 8, 9, 10 © 2007 Tim Soter
Foreword by Adam Moss

All rights reserved. No part of this publication may be reproduced, stored in a retrieval
system, or transmitted in any form or by any
means, electronic, mechanical, photocopying,
recording, or otherwise, without prior consent of
publishers.

09 08 07   10 9 8 7 6 5 4 3 2 1

First Edition

Printed in China

ISBN-13: 978-1-59591-036-3

Library of Congress Control Number:
2007924107

Images on the following pages previously published by New York Magazine: 18–19, 21, 23,
24–25, 27, 35, 37, 38–41,49, 50, 53, 54–55, 61,
65, 70, 74, 76–79, 81, 84–85, 88–89, 90, 97–99,
101, 106, 109, 111, 115, 116, 119, 121, 123, 125,
127, 133, 139, 141, 142, 144–145, 147, 149, 158,
160, 168, 172, 184, 189, 201, 209, 214, 219, 223.
All other images were created from digital files
provided by Picturehouse.

NEW YORK

—

LOOK
BOOK

—

A GALLERY OF STREET FASHION

by *Amy Larocca* & *Jake Chessum*

MELCHER
MEDIA

FOREWORD

—

BY

ADAM MOSS

EDITOR-IN-CHIEF

NEW YORK MAGAZINE

Y ou see them everywhere, strutting up and down the New York streets, flaunting their style like plumage. As you try hard not to stare, you can't help but admire their taste, or courage, or both. Perhaps you've wanted to stop them, grab them by their purple neon lapels, and ask them just what they were thinking when they got dressed that morning. What if we did the stopping for you? That was the genesis of the Look Book.

Jody Quon, *New York* magazine's photography director, chose Jake Chessum to take the pictures. His photographic style was so animated you could feel his subjects in mid-stride. We paired him with Amy Larocca, the magazine's fashion writer, and sent them out, armed with release forms, a portable white backdrop and our hopes that this exercise might actually yield some interesting results.

As it turned out, they were a perfect match. Amy and Jake discovered they shared a talent for choosing—and seducing—just the right subjects for this social experiment. And what they brought back turned out to be richer and more wonderful than we'd imagined. We knew the city was full of stylish people—this is a world fashion capital, after all. What we didn't realize was the depth of personality that each style revealed. There were plenty of women and men wearing the latest fashions, but the streets also randomly generated legions of incredible-looking people who'd given serious thought to making their look their own. Everybody has to run to the corner for milk or cat food; I don't think we realized just how many people dressed for the occasion.

After each shoot, we pored over the film. There we'd discover a home nurse sporting pink thigh-high boots, an FIT student with hair magnetically pulled to the heavens, two young cousins bursting with pride in their natty, impeccable suits. Our debut Look Book subject was the elegant doyenne Thelma Schnitzer (pages 220–221), speaking in a cadence that uncannily mirrored the precision of her look. It almost always works like that—people sound just the way they look. Amy's questions are respectfully impertinent. She draws responses from her subjects that are remarkable for their candor. The pictures are posed, yet the portraits are candid in the truest sense of the term.

When we began publishing the Look Book, the reaction was electric and, at least initially, polarizing. Some thought we were condescending, when our intent was exactly the opposite. Regardless, the Look Book became the most popular destination in the new incarnation of the magazine, dissected and parsed each week on blogs, in newspapers, and at cocktail parties. In time, people saw what we saw: that what began as a lighthearted examination of style on the streets became something more anthropological.

We called it the Look Book to echo the name designers give to their compilations of a season's collection. After all, it is our frequently-made contention that the streets of New York are a giant runway, with each passerby playing the role of model and designer of his own style. But we also thought that one day Jake and Amy's project might make a good book—a Look Book book. And so it has.

INTRODUCTION

—

BY

AMY LAROCCA & JAKE CHESSUM

When we tell people that we're the team behind the Look Book, we get a predictable response. "Would I make it?" everyone wants to know. People throw up their hands and a mixture of pride and insecurity flushes their cheeks. "Could I be in the Look Book?" The answer, always, is maybe. Our interest isn't necessarily in the outlandish or extreme—though hot pants in February are hard to resist. The Look Book is also about subtlety and nuance. After spending many afternoons staking out street corners, we've learned that style in New York is a language all its own. You can tell a lot about a banker from the cuff of his shirt, or about an NYU student from her Hermès scarf, or about an artist from the mounds of old mascara lining his eyes.

The other question we're always asked is, "How do you find these people?" Here's how: For the past three years, about once a month, we set up a temporary studio somewhere in New York. We never tell anyone where or when we're going (though we've been offered all sorts of things—a Porsche, for example—for the information). We wait and we watch for someone to catch our eye. One fine October morning, we saw a pair of especially green jeans heading down the stairs to the Union Square subway station. We quickly realized that the fantastic jeans were attached to John Waters and gave chase. At first he didn't want to be photographed; in his eyes, Look Book's greatness was its celebration of the unknown, the unfamous, the

JAKE AND AMY WORK ON PRINCE STREET, IN SOHO.

unused-to-being-photographed. He had a point, but we countered that the Look Book is a documentary of New York's streets, and John Waters is as much part of that landscape as Crystal Boria (70–71), Duane Littles (114–115), or Janice Su carrying her beloved, ball-jointed doll (166–167). He said yes.

It's rare that someone says no when approached for the Look Book; generally, our subjects are flattered. Even Helen Mirren let us snap her when we found her walking down Prince Street one day (although she later declined the interview!). We're fast, too—the time lapse between Amy's approach and Jake's click of the shutter is two minutes at most. Occasionally, though, we've been mistaken for panhandlers or purse snatchers. One woman in a matching fur coat and hat said to Amy, "Oh, you want to take my picture? I thought you were a little beggar girl."

We have a theory on why people are so willing to stop and pose: Being in the Look Book is a chance to introduce yourself to the city. "Here I am, something worth capturing, preserving, publishing in a magazine." Sometimes, the outfits are tremendously successful; other times, they're puzzlingly out of sync with their explanation, and that conflict is what intrigues. But quite often, they're spot on. "I'm quite successful," the banker's cuffs say, "and I've been to Europe."

The subjects of the Look Book are a happy accident. Their style, however, is not.

LEFT: THE CORNER OF PRINCE STREET. *RIGHT:* THE CORNER OF MADISON AVENUE AND 61ST STREET.

THE
LOOKS

JANICZA BRAVO
Director

How long have you had a shaved head?
Ever since I graduated from NYU in 2003.
I was graduating, and I had broken up
with someone and I wanted something
new. It's been four years, and I love it.

Is it easy to maintain?
I shave my head every day. I'm pretty
persistent about it. There are times when
I don't, if I'm really busy or out of the
country or something like that.

What's your style?
My style is very much rooted in *Annie
Hall.* Also, I tend to like older things:
Mostly everything I wear is vintage. It's
very masculine, but every once in a while
something very feminine.

What kind of name is Janicza?
It's Polish actually. I'm not Polish, as you
can probably tell. My parents are from
Panama, which is where I was raised, and
I think for a really long time my mother
thought she made it up. There are a lot
of crazy names in Panama; it's a nexus of
all different cultures. But then in college I
took a Russian Avant Garde theater class
and my teacher said my name correctly.
I was confused because he was Anglo,
but he explained that it's an old Eastern
European name.

Where do you live?
I live in Williamsburg. It's sort of a hotbed
of youth culture—cool, fun, hip, that stuff.
I wouldn't really choose to live anywhere
else right now because I like seeing people
my own age who are very attractive. There
are throngs of youth everywhere, and I
really enjoy that.

How do you put your outfits together?
When I was younger I would spend a
couple of hours a night trying things on,
but now I'm much more comfortable with
what my style is, so it doesn't take me that
long. But if there's an event, or I'm, say,
meeting up with an ex, I want to be super
executed but in a casual way. I used to iron
every day. I've been ironing every day since
I was thirteen, but I've calmed down a bit.
I guess I have a slight case of OCD.

JULIA ERDMAN
NYU Sophomore

What's your major?
French lit. And I also have internships at Alessandro Dell'Acqua and Claire Oliver Fine Art.

You must be very busy.
I make time! I figure if you don't go to bed exhausted, you're doing something wrong. My friends are always like, "Julia, if you ever come to school in sweatpants, then we'll know you've pushed yourself too far."

You've never gone to class in sweatpants?
Never. I dress like this all the time.

Where did it all come from?
The green coat is from Barneys, the most recent fall collection. The turtleneck is Celine. The scarf speaks for itself—Hermès. The skirt is vintage Genny. My mother actually found it for me. I had to get it shortened a bit, but now I wear it all the time. The flats are Louis, and the bag is the same. Just a classic. The sunglasses are Gucci, and I made the stupid mistake of getting transition lenses. Now, when I go inside, I have this stupid sunglass thing.

Do your parents give you a clothing allowance?
I earn most of my own money. They give me money to feed myself, but, of course, you never really spend your money the way your parents want.

What do you think of the Olsen sisters?
People dress how they are. If that's their look, then, hey, so be it. I did see one of them—I don't know which one's which—at Bungalow 8 with Bob Saget.

Who are your style icons?
Audrey Hepburn, Maria Callas, that librarian from *The Mummy* [Rachel Weisz]. I don't know who she is, but I saw her on TV and I was like, "She's fabulous!"

Where are you from?
Palo Alto, but my parents live in Las Vegas now. My dad is in investments—it's one of those things where I don't really know what he does. My mom's retired, but she loves the casinos, so it works out.

What are you going to do with that French-lit degree?
The dream job would be restaurant critic at the *New York Times*. I'm a culture-phile, but I definitely think that food comes first—then art, then fashion.

How's the NYU cafeteria food?
I haven't eaten it in a very long time. You're required to in your freshman year, but I didn't even eat it then.

TROY ARCAND
Bartender

Tell me about your style.
Oh, I don't know. I read all these magazines where people have these funny little things to say about themselves and I'm like, who comes up with these things? I'm dressed like a fool all the time. I don't have just one theme. One day I might dress like a robot, but the next day might be cowboy.

Well, that's a funny little thing, no?
But it's not like some quirky thing I've been thinking of for years, just waiting for some quirky girl to come take my picture on Bedford Avenue.

Do you spend much time thinking about your outfit in the morning?
No. The thought happens when you're buying things. Once something makes it home, I've already put in the thought.

As a bartender, you must hear lots of people's stories.
It's not so bad at wd-50, where I work now, because most of the people at the bar aren't there alone. I bartended at some other bars that were more low-end, but I'm so bad at small talk that people can always tell I'm not listening, which is really sad. I'm not interested in other people's problems.

What's the weirdest thing anyone's told you?
Well, people always say I must be from Boston because of my accent, but I'm from Providence, Rhode Island. But one night Brooke Shields came in and sat at the bar and we started chatting and she immediately said, "Hey, you're from Providence." She's the only one who ever got it right.

Do you like having the accent?
I love it. It's fantastic. People think it's amazing, but it's just Providence plus public school education, that's all.

MICA DE JESUS
Gypsy

What do gypsies do?
Well, I paint. I sing. I dance. I read tarot cards. I write. I make collages. My family is, like, traveling, wandering vagabond people. It's not like being a hippie or something. You can decide to be a hippie. If you're a gypsy, it's just who you are.

How do you support yourself?
I find odd jobs here and there. My friend also makes little polymer-clay figures, and he sells them in the park. I help him out because people are attracted to the way that I look.

Tell me about this look.
Usually it's spontaneous. I have some clothes, and I like colors. Instead of wearing just one thing that matches one color in the skirt, I'll wear a couple of things that match a couple of colors in the skirt.

Is dressing a form of expression for you?
Yes. People tell me that they can tell that I'm easygoing, that I'm pretty cool, that I'm a chill person to talk to. I'm guessing that's because nobody else has the style that I wear because it's my own—not something that came out of Wet Seal.

What's the jewelry on your forehead?
That's an earring. I found it on the subway. That's something I really like about New York: There's a lot of stuff to find. You tend to only find one earring at a time, though. So I stick them in my hair.

DR. ROSALIE MISHKIN
Psychologist

How would you describe your personal style?
I never think about it! This jacket is about 35 years old, and the hat's about six years old. I just try to conceal the fact that I'm basically dressed comfortably all the time, but people stop me on the street three to four times a week to tell me I look beautiful.

Do you work out?
I'm a member of the Peninsula Spa. I work on the elliptical trainer, and I've been doing Pilates, and I've found that I have some talent for tap dancing. If you saw me, you would crack up. Anything my teacher can do, I can do it, pretty much.

You're very well-groomed.
I do take a lot of care with my makeup. I get my nails done regularly, and I like to coordinate colors.

What are your favorite products?
I like the Perricone face-firming activator and the Estée Lauder double-wear concealer. Some of my products are very inexpensive—my eyebrow pencil and lip liner are Prestige, from Duane Reade. You see, it's all very here, there, and wherever! The foundation I'm using is Paula Dorf. People come up to me and say I have such wonderful skin, but I have terrible skin. What I do have is a good visual sense.

Where do you shop?
I don't like to shop. I buy many things from catalogues. I like Lands' End and Leon Levin golf shirts and New Balance sneakers.

How long have you been a psychologist?
I've been in practice for, oh, my goodness, 40 years, fifteen in London.

Do Brits and Americans have different neuroses?
The defenses are different, but the symptoms are the same. All of us are trying to be connected to other people, and so much of the frustration is being unable to do it. What I do is about repairing the ability to connect with others through this trusting process—first trusting me and then trusting yourself.

What can you tell about your patients from the way they look?
Mostly, you read people by the facial expression and enthusiasm and sparkle that they emanate. If you feel empowered, you carry yourself well. My daughter doesn't care much for clothes, but she has tremendous style because she has her own presence. That comes from a good role model in the mother.

You're very well-groomed.
I do take a lot of care with my makeup. I get my nails done regularly, and I like to coordinate colors.

What do you do?
I'm second-in-command of the union for
the whole New York City Department of
Corrections—Rikers, the court facilities,
the prison hospitals.

**If you're going to prison in New York,
which one should you hope for?**
No prison.

How would you describe your style?
Mature conservative. A little bit of the old,
a little bit of the new. My family originated
in the South, but I'm from Harlem, so
that's where I get some of my style. The
hat is from a haberdashery by City Hall.
The suit is from Portobello, and the shoes
are Stacy Adams.

What do you think of prison style?
I don't really believe in the fashion of
having the baggy pants hanging down. I
don't think it's appropriate to show the
underwear. We have female wardens—it's
disrespectful.

Do you like the crime shows on TV?
What everybody needs to know is that
jail is a city within a city. Everything that
happens outside happens inside too.

PETE KRESS

Bouncer, with Seamus,
his pit bull

Do you like being a bouncer?
It's a job. I work at Sin-é on Attorney Street, and it's pretty low-key there. But at other places, I've had fights, people slapping their girlfriends, all that stuff. I don't really get angry, I just tell them they've got to cut it out. I'm also a photographer.

How would you describe your style?
Rico Suave? An all-American can't-do attitude? I think if someone could encapsulate your style in a phrase— well, I don't know how I'd feel about that person. I just keeps it real.

Where do you shop?
Pop's Popular Clothing in beautiful Greenpoint, Brooklyn, or Iceberg Army-Navy. I like work clothes and Army surplus because they're sturdy. I don't like cheap clothes that you wear for a couple months and then they're all messed up.

How many tattoos do you have?
I never really counted. I started getting them before it was even legal. You'd have to go up to some dude's apartment. Some are designs that I like. Some are representative of events, like anniversaries or trips that I've taken.

What kind of pictures do you take?
I see a lot of crazy shit, so I started carrying a camera 'cause I'm always like, No one's going to believe this. If I see crazy people carrying pig carcasses on Stanton Street, which I did, I take their picture.

What made you get a pit bull?
I was thinking about a German shepherd. But when I saw this guy on Petfinder, he was just so adorable. He's not aggressive, but a lot of people think pit bulls are super-mean. People are definitely more hesitant about approaching me than they would be if I had a teacup poodle.

What do you think about CBGB's closing?
It should stay open as a historical landmark, but CBGB hasn't been relevant in twenty years.

Where do you think punk lives now?
I really don't think it exists anymore. It's about as relevant as kids dressing up as hippies.

ALEX KENNEDY-GRANT
Musician

What are you up to today?
I'm basically enjoying the fine fall afternoon and going to get a copy of *Wax Poetics*. It's a magazine about funk, soul, jazz. It's academic-ish.

It's late afternoon. Do you not have a job?
Not currently. I'm just borrowing money from people who love me.

So you're a musician?
I'm a guitar player, a front man. I sing all of my own songs and I play the guitar. Nobody really plays the guitar anymore. It's almost like if you know what you're doing and you are a virtuoso, it puts you at a disadvantage. But I'm a virtuoso, and I don't hide that fact.

Does that mean you haven't been signed?
Yeah. I'm totally independent. But I'd like to get paid to make records because playing music is the only thing I really dig.

What's your music like?
It's psychedelic soul and blues-rock stuff. I like music where you're not afraid of different styles.

Let's talk about your hair.
I've had long hair in various forms since high school. I've had dreadlocks a couple of times. This phase has been going on for a couple of years.

How do you care for it?
A couple of times a week I wash it. It's curly. It's big. And since I just woke up, you're seeing it in a totally raw state. Not that the unraw state looks very different.

CHANTAL ADAIR
Student

What are you listening to?
Gwen Stefani. That new song of hers, the stupid little poppy one.

Do you have style icons?
Victoria Beckham. She's always so put together. I grew up listening to the Spice Girls. I always liked how she'd be the one in the little black dress.

What do you do?
I study art history. I really like contemporary art, or modern, as some people say, like Cubism, Kandinsky, Marc Chagall. I've been studying for almost two years. Before that, I was modeling.

Why did you stop?
I didn't like how the industry treats young models. It was just like being in a flock, really. I didn't like how you get no respect unless you're one of the top girls. And it really hurts your self-esteem. Studying art history is much better.

How did you get into modeling?
I was really awkward and geeky in high school. I was on the basketball team, and I didn't have any friends. My sister entered me in the *Cosmo* model search because she felt really sad for me.

Tell me about your style.
I like black a lot, but that's left over from high school. I didn't like to be noticed.

Do you like being noticed now?
Definitely. I'm not as awkward as I used to be.

What's the next trend?

Right now I'm trying to cross up early eighties Bronx B-boy style with Tokyo, and then top it off with a Parisian thing, so it's like the International B-boy.

MICHAEL D'ANDRADE
Fashion Forecaster

What does it mean that you're a fashion forecaster?

I'm into everything: fashion, music, video games, as everyone else is, but I try to be up on the next trend, be the alpha male. I see lots of kids who are like the beta version of me.

What's the next trend?

Right now I'm trying to cross up early eighties Bronx B-boy style with Tokyo, and then top it off with a Parisian thing, so it's like the International B-boy. But right now, if you wear Tsubi jeans and pointy sneakers, that might be good, but it'll be up in Harlem next season. Downtown is way ahead of uptown.

Are you from downtown?

Born and raised on Delancey and Pitt.

How much has your neighborhood changed?

There's no difference between the Lower East Side and Soho anymore. You can't just, like, go and have lunch on Clinton Street without it being all fancified. I used to DJ, and I remember being so excited that there were places in my neighborhood, but now it's spring break every night, with drunk white people on every curb screaming. If I were to go to, like, Michigan or whatever, I'd hang out and have a good time, but I wouldn't try to act like a native. I'd try to respect other people's cities.

Do you have real lenses in those glasses?

With all my Cazals and all my Guccis, I don't get my prescription put in.

Why is there so much retro fashion right now?

Because trends move too fast. You've got to go back and finish it up. Back in the day my friend and I tried to kill it on the retro scale, like acid-washed fanny packs. Kids used to clown me on the train for it, but then mass media puts it into perspective and everyone does it.

OLEG CASSINI
Fashion Designer

What are you wearing today?

I have the jeans specifically made for me, because if not, why bother? I love animals and I hate to wear a leather jacket, but if you're going to wear a leather jacket, it's just got to be right. And nobody can do it better than a designer who's designing for himself. Look, it's the best leather there is. One of the secrets to being in good shape is to keep your head warm. This hat I use for golf, and it is fantastic. With shoes, I have a fetish. They have to be beautiful. These are short Italian boots by Tanino Crisci. I have maybe 50 pairs of shoes of classical beauty. I look at them most of the time, but I do not wear them. I have a passion for shoes.

How old are you now?

They are always exaggerating, but the fact is that I am 91 going on 92.

You're in great shape. Do you have any advice?

I have plenty of advice! You could write a whole column on my advice! Assuming what you say—that I look great—is correct, I will tell you that I do watch what I eat. Quantity is the No. 1 factor. And what I eat, that is No. 2. Everybody by now knows what one should eat; the problem is that the portions are unnecessary. And I always live a life of competitive sport. I still play tennis, I still play golf, and I have three saddle horses to ride in the country.

You've spent your life designing for other people. How would you describe your own style?

I can afford to have the most stylish clothes because I am slim! I'm 30 in the waist. The proportion in my shoulder and hips is that of a very athletic, young guy. I'm just athletic, not young, but the great illusion is there because I am so slim.

Whose style do you love?

There I will refuse to play ball with you. I just think about what I like: style, fit, quality. I'm not preoccupied by other people.

Where are you going today?

I go off to La Houppa on 64th Street for lunch. They make special things for me, special foods. The difference between living to 100 and living to 60 is really one of management. I think I'm a pretty good manager, don't you?

You've spent your life designing for other people. How would you describe your own style?

I can afford to have the most stylish clothes because I am slim!

JON REIGLE
Freak-Show Performer

Tell me about the horns.
Mine are done out of virgin-grade Teflon,
second generation. I used to have implants
up to the fourth set; they were a lot bigger.
But I got in trouble because I worked in a
bar and I was going through a weird time
and I let people get to me too much, so
I took them out. It's based on Pan from
Greek mythology. People assume it's about
the devil, but it's not.

How long did it take you to do your ears?
Six or seven years. If you don't go slow,
they just blow out and you wind up losing
a lobe. But I'm more focused on my tattoos
right now.

What's your favorite?
My face. I actually figure that all these
tattoos have made me a better person.
When I did my face it was, like, people are
going to want to talk to me. And I have to
be okay with that.

HOLLY HARNSONGKRAM
*Creative Director and Part Owner of
Nom de Guerre*

What are you wearing?
The hat is from an Army and Navy store in
Paris, the coat is A.P.C. The scarf is from
the Annex flea market on 26th Street, and
the jeans are also A.P.C. They're called
"The New Standard." The boots are, like,
ages old. They're Marc Jacobs.

Any makeup?
I usually buy lip gloss from Fresh. It's got
a lot of natural ingredients. For perfume, I
wear Creed's Silver Mountain Water.

**Nom de Guerre sells high-end sneakers
and avant-garde design. What exactly
does a creative director do there?**
I set up the look and the concept, which
is a streamlined version of an Army and
Navy store, just essential pieces, exactly
what you'd need to get along in the city.

So is your own look pretty streamlined?
It's not girlie or anything. I prefer just
getting dressed as opposed to thinking
about it too much.

What are you doing on Madison Avenue?
I'm running around and getting
inspiration. Usually it comes from Chelsea
art galleries. I'll see a color or a texture
that translates into clothing that I need.
I saw these really great paintings with
halftone prints today.

**Do books and movies do that for
you, too?**
Well, nothing in the theaters. Right now,
I'm having my own Godard, early New
Wave moment.

**Are there any trends that you really can't
stand?**
You can get inspiration from pretty much
anyone and anything. I mean, if I go out
and listen to a band, there will be some
girl there wearing leg warmers that
were meant for, like, duck hunting. I
just like watching people and seeing
what they wear.

Even velour tracksuits?
I'm not that difficult. Just keep your
underwear in the proper place. None of
those weird thong things coming out the
top. But I'm not turned off by anyone's
personal style, because to me, it all makes
sense. Sociologically, it gives you a good
idea of what their background is, and what
their interests are.

**So what can we learn about you from
your outfit?**
I have absolutely no idea. I'd rather not
go there.

SUZANNE
Dog Walker

Why only one name?
I'm more comfortable that way. My very
close friends know my last name, but I
don't really share it. I'm pretty distinct-
looking, so if you know Suzanne, then you
just know.

How did you get into dog walking?
Some people can learn skills to work with
dogs, but for me it's just not that difficult.
I have a really deep connection with my
dogs—they really vibe on my energy. I feel
their vibe, they feel my vibe.

Tell me about your look.
There's a part of me that's extremely
feminine and another part that's
masculine. I'm into the whole primitive-
tribal thing when I make jewelry, but I
also love false eyelashes, tons of makeup,
stilettos, and corsets. It really depends on
what I'm doing, the weather, my mood,
and whether or not I'm taking a cab.

**What kind of makeup are you
wearing today?**
It's all about the foundation. I'm currently
using M.A.C. I love it. The makeup is
great quality, and the colors are just so
saturated. But really, what you have to do
is moisturize. I have a whole drawer, and
I switch up depending on my skin's needs.
Vitamin E oil usually does the trick.

What else do you do?
I was in an all-female hardcore-slash-
punk band, and I'm currently playing
drums for a new project. We haven't
picked a name yet, but whatever it is, I'm
sure the sound will be pure insanity.

PETER HAYN
Artist

What kind of artist are you?
I do a little sculpturing and painting.
Dabbling. I'm not a professional, I'm a
retired old man. I actually trained as an
economist in Germany prior to my arrival
here in New York.

When did you come here?
The year Marilyn Monroe died [1962].
And it was strictly adventurous, not a
typical immigrant story. I liked New
York—it was a fun place in the sixties and
seventies. The city really embraced my
lifestyle.

What kind of lifestyle is that?
I've lived a will-o'-the-wisp life. There
was a lot of international travel, and then
I did all sorts of things in between just to
finance my travels. I worked for a German
corporation, for a restaurant, as an
executive assistant—whatever came up.

Where did you travel?
You name it. I went to Rio a couple of
times, Thailand numerous times, and to
India, of course, but that was just to see
the Taj Mahal. And to Egypt to see the
pyramids, and Iraq in 1968 because I
wanted to see the Hanging Gardens.

Have you seen all the Seven Wonders?
Yes. And it was when I saw the ticker-tape
parades in New York on TV that I wanted
to come here.

Where do you live?
I live in a very historic building called the
Ansonia on the Upper West Side. I have
lived there since 1977, to be exact, and now
I couldn't afford it.

Is your rent in the three figures?
Of course! I don't pay $90 a month!

I meant, is it under a thousand?
Absolutely, it is.

Where did you get this outfit?
This is my least favorite coat. I have fifteen
fur coats, and I wish I'd met you on one
of my other strolls up and down Madison
Avenue. There are so many others that
are more exciting or eye-catching. But I
bought this one at Alexander Ross on East
59th Street, which no longer exists. And
it's just a little black silk scarf and a black
Eric Javits hat from Saks.

How would you describe your style?
I don't want to blow my own horn, but do
you know Quentin Crisp? *The Naked Civil
Servant?*

**You see yourself as a German
Quentin Crisp?**
Well, yes.

TERRANCE BARTON
High-School Student

KAY GOLDBERG
Ninth Grader

How would you describe your personal style?

Fantastically random slash colorful. But I mean, black is the best color even though it's not a color. I like black, but I'm not super-black, all negativity and whatever.

Where did you get this outfit?

I got my shoes at, I don't know, a Converse store? My rainbow tights came from this vintage boutique called Hidden Treasures in Topanga, California. My mom got the vest for me at this awesome place on Greenwich Avenue called Zachary's Smile. The parka is from Cover Up on Macdougal Street.

So you really like vintage?

They definitely got it right in the past. Some of the things now are just being exotic for the sake of being exotic.

Exotic?

Well, I love stuff that doesn't look like you would love it, but then you look at it and it turns out you do love it. I don't like stuff that's trying too hard.

Do you think the West Village has changed a lot?

It's always going to be the Village, by which I mean it's basically the single greatest place in the world, but I think it has changed. Where there used to be a random little place where people will sell their own jewelry, now there's, like, Ralph Lauren. It seems more like a place to be than a place where you are.

Who are your style heroes?

Generally, people who care about the message of their clothing. My white T-shirt just looks like a white T-shirt, but it's by American Apparel, and they have a no-sweatshop policy.

Your dad's a record executive. What music do you love?

I love the Doors. I absolutely love the Doors. I love the Ramones. For current music, I like the Killers. I really like the Strokes: They definitely rock. The Pixies rock. The Libertines are amazing. And the Clash. But I mean, obviously.

Do you want to be a musician?

Music is the absolute biggest thing in my life. I play piano and guitar, and I'm learning bass. Ideally, I want to grow up to be a rock star.

A rock star like who?

I would be like Mozart. He rocked. He was the biggest rock star in the world. Close tie with Jim Morrison. Now my mom is rolling her eyes.

Exotic?
Well, I love stuff that doesn't look like you would love it, but then you look at it and it turns out you do love it. I don't like stuff that's trying too hard.

KIM JOHNSON
Showroom Sales Manager

What's the best fashion advice you've ever gotten?

Not to wear what's cool but to wear what you actually like. I'm a little older now, and I think I'm figuring it out. I used to follow every trend out there. Also: no cheap stuff. That doesn't work either.

Nice tuxes.
It's difficult for people like us to wear a tux without thinking about Sean Connery. But Sean Connery is here! And he's dressed more like Bono.

KAREN MANN
Personal Shopper

What kinds of things do you shop for?

My whole belief is chic and cheap. This necklace, this shirt: H&M, can you believe it? And the pants and shoes are from the Gap. Many people think those stores are inappropriate for someone my age, but if you're selective, it can really work. I don't wear designer clothes anymore.

Why not?

It's a financial thing, but also it just made me feel old. My friends and I all agree: Designer clothes make us look like matrons.

What are your clients like?

Personal shopping is all word of mouth. My clients tend to be 40 years of age and up, and what I try to do is teach them that style is not about price—it just has to do with knowing your look.

Does your husband have good style?

When I married him, he said, "I don't wear brown." I didn't understand that. So now he wears brown all the time, and I guess it's okay, because we've been married for 44 years and we're best friends.

Any tips for aging gracefully?

I have not had plastic surgery. Well, not yet. I do heavy weights just once a week for fifteen minutes. No gym, no sweating. And slather on body lotion with SPF. I'd been scouring the city for a good one forever, and I finally found it at Fairway, in the organic aisle. It's a brand called Alba, and you can get a quart-size bottle for $20, with an SPF of sixteen. It's my obsession.

What kinds of things do you shop for?

My whole belief is chic and cheap. I don't wear designer clothes anymore.

JOHN WATERS
Filmmaker

What are you up to today?
I'm going to have lunch with Margo Lions, who's one of the main producers of *Hairspray* on Broadway.

Do you always ride the subway?
People always ask me what I'm doing on the subway, but I love it! Sometimes I like to ride in the front car and look out the window at the rats. I'm just glad I'm not crippled, because I hate the bus. Every block takes a hundred hours.

Do you get recognized much?
I don't always look up. But I'm nice to everyone who makes eye contact, unless they're singing with a cup. People are usually so nice. Sometimes they just mouth "Thank you!" and I love it. It makes me feel like Oprah.

How long have you had that mustache?
Since I was 19, and I'm 60 now. I was a yippie agitator, and I wanted to look like Little Richard. I dressed like a hippie pimp back then, because punk wasn't around yet. I guess I've never fit in my own minority. It's been a lifelong problem. Or, to look at it another way, it's been a career.

Tell me about your look.
My whole look is "disaster at the dry cleaner." Usually it's Japanese. Today I'm wearing Ray-Bans that I got in a gift bag, and a Brooks Brothers watch. I'm really furious about the watch because I've bought the same one every ten years forever and I just found out it's been discontinued. I'm wearing turquoise 501 Levi's.

How about the jacket?
It's Comme des Garçons. And a Paul Smith scarf and socks, and a Brooks Brothers turtleneck. I've got Junya Watanabe sneakers and Gap boxer shorts on.

Any cologne?
Odeur 53 men's cologne from Comme des Garçons. It smells like bug repellent.

Is this a standard outfit for you?
Yes, because when I got dressed I was thinking that I wasn't going to have to be John Waters today. If I did, I would have on more ludicrous things.

Any style icons?
Rufus Wainwright always has a look. Joan Kennedy always looks startling. Kate Moss has never looked bad in her life. And the *Jackass* boys. If ever there was a gang of boys I could hang out with and get fashion lessons from, it's them. And, oh! Kitty Carlisle Hart.

Do you get recognized much?
People are usually so nice. Sometimes they just mouth "Thank you!" and I love it. It makes me feel like Oprah.

JONATHAN "FLI GUY" SAUNDERS, TYQUAN "YOUNG MONEY" JONIES, ERICK "SOCKS" JONIES, AND DERRON "RONNEY FRESH" BOND
The "Fli High Fli Guys"

What's this style?

FLI GUY: Our whole style is basically geek style. Like we got stuffed in a locker because we're real smart and the lenses of our glasses get knocked out.

How'd you come up with it?

FLI GUY: We were watching *The Fresh Prince of Bel-Air*, and Will Smith had some weird style in, like, '86, '87. We were like, Damn! We do the same shit just like him! And then we saw how he and Jazzy Jeff had a handshake, so we incorporated that and now we're the Fli High Fli Guys, a.k.a. the Fresh Princes.

You must get a lot of attention.

RONNEY FRESH: Let me put it this way: The whole world is a fashion show to us. If other people get the attention, that's no good.

What music are you listening to?

FLI GUY: Jazz. A whole lot of opera. 'Cause it's real soothing.

How'd you come up with it?

We were watching *The Fresh Prince of Bel-Air,* and Will Smith had some weird style in, like, '86, '87. We were like, Damn! We do the same shit just like him!

FRANK "BUTCH THE HAT" AQUILINO
Actor

CYNTHIA ROWLEY
Designer

Where are you going today?
To lunch at Pastis with an editor at *Vogue*.

What are you wearing?
The dress is about eight years old—it's vintage Cynthia Rowley! The belt is this season, the stockings were last fall, and the shoes and the bag are next fall. The jacket is by my friend Gary Graham. He's a designer who makes these cool leather jackets and then washes them so they get all shrunken and worn-looking. People are always telling me I have a rip in my sleeve, and I say, "No, it's supposed to be like that."

Do you always wear your own clothes?
Only because I get embarrassed if people ask me and I'm not. Like these shoes, which I'm totally obsessed about—some lady pulled up in a taxi and said, "Where did you get those shoes?" It would be too embarrassing to say, "Louboutin!" "Marc Jacobs!" Plus I like to resuscitate my old stuff, you know, put the defibrillator paddles on an old black dress.

If you were to wear other designers, who would you wear?
I do wear a lot of vintage. I guess I would like a little bit from a lot of different designers. European, mostly. Bill, my boyfriend, did just buy me some Prada shoes, which I thought was the most romantic thing in the world.

Who would you like to see in your clothes?
In my personal clothes? Brad Pitt. I would've liked to have dressed John DeLorean in the seventies, but I guess I'm a little late for that.

What beauty products do you use?
I use Redken Water Wax in my hair every day. I can't leave the house without it. And then I usually just wake up in the morning and don't put on any makeup, just sunglasses. I drop my daughter off at school, and when I get to work I do makeup—eyeliner, mascara, and lipstick. I have my own makeup that's sold in Japan only, and I use that, but I love Vincent Longo's Pearl Berry lipstick and L'Oréal Voluminous Mascara.

Your office used to be in the garment district. Are you glad you moved to the West Village?
I was standing on the corner the other day and this mother and daughter were saying, "I love you 1600 percent," "I love you a million percent," and I thought, that just does not happen on 40th and Seventh.

Do you always wear your own clothes?
Only because I get embarrassed if people ask me and I'm not.

ROBERT MCKNIGHT
Retiree

GENTRY DAYTON
Shopclerk

KATE YOUNG
Stylist

What's your look?
I would say Goth Victoriana
Governess. Sometimes I look kind
of "Mommy drinks."

Who inspires you?
My favorite style of anyone in the world
is the really skinny woman named
Margaret [Margit Carstensen] in all of
Fassbinder's films.

Why's that?
She's just really, really skinny! I love her.
And I love Charlotte Rampling, but the
Charlotte Rampling of the seventies.

Where did you get this outfit?
The coat is vintage—I bought it at Niagara
Falls Family Thrift. The T-shirt is Rogan,
and the jeans are by Loomstate, made
from organic cotton. You can get both
of them at Steven Alan. My shoes are
Christian Louboutin. And I'm wearing
Dolce & Gabbana socks with roses
on them. I have a passion for Dolce &
Gabbana and Missoni socks. Also, I have
on vintage Christian icons by Miracle
Icons. You can get them at Barneys.

How long has your hair been platinum?
Two years in January. Andre at Orlando
Pita salon colors it. Mark Townsend,
celebrity hairstylist extraordinaire, cuts
it. He's from L.A., but when he comes to
town for the Olsen twins, he stops by my
house.

What made you do it?
I cut my hair way too short and didn't feel
cute, so I thought if I bleached it white,
I'd look like Madonna on the cover of the
True Blue album.

Do people treat you differently now?
When I travel for work—last week I was
in Wisconsin—people stare. And when
I have roots, people uptown think I'm
dirty. They're not so nice to me in shops
and restaurants, because I look Courtney
Love–ish.

**What are you doing for the holidays this
year?**
Home to Pennsylvania. My dad cooks, and
on Thanksgiving everyone wears weird
hats. I bought a cheese hat in Wisconsin.

What do you want for Christmas?
Thorn earrings from Ted Muehling, and
some Victorian mourning jewelry from
Doyle & Doyle. Last year, my boyfriend
gave me a still from Lansing-Dreiden's "A
Sectioned Beam" video, and that was the
best present ever.

What are you giving?
I can't tell!

What's your look?
I would say Goth
Victoriana Governess.
Sometimes I look
kind of "Mommy
drinks."

TINA PINA
Artist and Musician

SAM MASTERS
High School Junior

How's high school?
Well, I'm at Browning but I'm also very much into acting, and I'm in a band called the Deadly Monks with two of my classmates. I'm the lead singer and bassist. School is school.

What kind of music do you listen to?
David Bowie. He's a musical genius and a trademark icon. I'm also very much into funky movie soundtracks, like *Dazed and Confused* and *Velvet Goldmine*. I like the band Spoon, and some old-school rap, too, like Run-DMC. And Bob Dylan—my dad's a huge Bob Dylan fan. We're just a big hippie family, really.

Tell me about your style.
I definitely like to funk it up. I love paisley, velvet jackets, tight jeans, and corduroys. I guess I just really love tight clothes. Onstage I sometimes wear a bit of eyeliner. Today I'm preppier because I didn't have much in my closet. The jacket I picked up at Urban Outfitters, and the tie I got in Paris last summer, just somewhere funky.

What kind of acting do you do?
Film. I've been working with the New York Film Academy, mainly in dramatic roles. You know, struggles with life, struggles with girlfriends. I like things very deep and very complex, like the movie *Closer*. One of my friends filmed a version of it, and I played the role of Jude Law. I love playing the mysterious characters.

Are you mysterious yourself?
Possibly. I definitely think I have a quirky side. I love to have fun, I'm very friendly, and I fall in love very easily. I have a girlfriend named Destine. I met her at one of my best friends' sweet sixteens. She goes to Dalton, and she's a big David Bowie fan. She's everything I've ever wanted.

CRYSTAL BORIA
Nursing Student

What are you doing today?

I'm coming from school, and, you know, I woke up feeling happy. I'm tired of wearing my uniform to school. I thought I'd dress really, really cute today.

Where did you get this outfit?

The pink boots I got from the Bronx at a little girly store. I don't remember the name. I like my shoes high. You never find me in sneakers or Tims. The jeans I bought, like, four years ago at Mony's: It's a clothing store in downtown Brooklyn on, like, Flatbush. They're made by Guess. My jacket, I bought it about a year ago. It was a little gift to myself, right around Christmas.

Whose style do you admire?

I like the way Beyoncé dresses. She had little shorts on with high pumps and a little belly shirt in one of her videos, and a lot of people said, "That's so revealing!" I thought it was cute. It's not revealing to me because I'm not scared. I know I've got a nice body, and this is how I dress. A lot of girls be giving me that look, like I stink. But I like shoes!

You must hate having to wear a uniform.

Well, I wouldn't be able to go to work like this unless my patients requested that I not wear a uniform. Sometimes they don't want their neighbors to know they have a nurse coming. So if that happens, then they're just going to have to deal with the way I dress! At my school, they don't allow you to wear nails, but I do like to get tips. I just go wherever I see Korean ladies.

What are your favorite movies?

There are two: *Scarface* and *Casino*. In *Scarface*, I don't like how he got to the top, but I know the strive. He started with nothing, and he got everything he wanted. And in *Casino*, it was like a dream come true, a knight in shining armor who sweeps you off your feet, and one day you're barely making it, and the next day you're so rich you don't know what to do. Both of them are about accomplishing what you want.

So what do you want?

I love *America's Next Top Model*, and I wish I could get the opportunity. I feel confident I could do it. I know they ask the girls to do difficult things, but I could do whatever. A girly-girl pose? Fine. And cut a shirt? I'm from Harlem! I cut shirts! I cut jeans! The things they ask the girls to do, I was like, we do that right here in Harlem. Always have.

IZZY ALGHANI
Musician

AMELIA PRESTON
Hairdresser and Makeup Artist

SOFIA HEDSTROM
Television Reporter

What do you do?

I'm a reporter for Swedish television based in New York. I cover everything from fashion to politics to sports.

What's your favorite type of story?

I did an interview with Karl Lagerfeld a few months ago, and that was really exciting. Also, I did a documentary on two old people and they were so amazing because they didn't censor themselves.

Are there subjects you don't enjoy?

I didn't think I liked sports, but I was at a hockey game in Detroit, and it was really exciting. Although I was covering Annika Sorenstam last week at the U.S. Open, and she didn't play well at all. Sports aren't fun if you are not covering a winner.

How would you describe your style?

I would say it's fun. I'm wearing shorts today, but if there are 365 days in a year, I wear a skirt 360 of them. I like to get dressed up in the morning. I love Viktor & Rolf, Anna Sui, and, of course, Karl Lagerfeld.

What do you think about the style of American newscasters?

I think, to be honest, they might be a little boring. They could use some more color. They could do something about that hair. They all have the same hair!

Where did you get this outfit?

The shorts I bought on sale at Banana Republic. They were perfect on the golf course. The shoes are from the East Village; the brand is Faryl Robin. And the socks are H&M. I think sixties style is going to be big for fall.

Being Swedish, do you wear lots of H&M?

Maybe I'm biased because I have so many friends who work there, but I think H&M is brilliant. Everyone has the opportunity to have style; it's not about having a million dollars. Maybe it has something to do with Sweden being a socialist country, but I love this concept.

Do New Yorkers have a lot of preconceptions about Swedish girls?

Of course! There's all that free-love stuff, but the most common question is, "Do you get everything for free?" And then they ask about Abba.

How would you describe your style?
I'm wearing shorts today, but if there are 365 days in a year, I wear a skirt 360 of them.

Is the collar only half-up on purpose?

That's the Linus in me. You know how the Berbers purposely weave a mistake into every rug? It's like that.

JOSH MILLER
*Commercial Director,
with Oskar, a soft-coated
wheaten terrier*

What would you call your style?
Someone described it to me perfectly once: *Details* meets circus clown.

Where did you get this outfit?
It's a Jack Spade hat. The hat and the tie really look Jack Spade, but don't make me sound like a fashion victim! My jacket is from a thrift store. The sweater's not thrift, it's Brooks Brothers. The jeans are Rogan. My watch is Panerai. I buy one watch every ten years, and I bought this one used, online, three years ago.

Is the collar only half-up on purpose?
That's the Linus in me. You know how the Berbers purposely weave a mistake into every rug? It's like that.

That's a very yellow bag.
It's from Coach, and it's a great color yellow—very obnoxious, in a subtle, tasteful sort of way.

How did you choose a wheaten terrier?
I'm allergic to dogs, and he's hypoallergenic.

Why'd you name him Oskar?
It was kind of an Oscar Wilde, Oscar the Grouch thing. But a friend had just named his kid Oscar, so I used the k out of good conscience.

He looks like he needs a lot of space. Do you have a giant apartment?
I live in a loft on Hudson Street, but I have this hundred-acre farm in Sullivan County. There's a pond and a stream and even more land than he needs. I bought it for Oskar. It was good for both of us.

What's your favorite commercial that you've ever made?
For the Mini Cooper. A duck shows up at a guy's apartment and they take a road trip.

How about your favorite all-time commercials?
I would say photography and movies inspire me more. I like Terrence Malick films; *The Thin Red Line* is my favorite. And *Gummo*.

Let me guess . . . you want to make movies?
Of course! It's kind of a cliché, though, huh?

LOUIS R. AIDALA
Attorney

How do you describe your style?
You're thinking that someone who looks like me deliberately does a certain style. I don't.

Not at all?
I will tell you about the shoes that I've got. They're called a. testoni, and they're made in Bologna. They just had to close their store on Fifth Avenue. The rents, they go crazy. Regular price, they're expensive. But I never pay regular price! At the going-out-of-business sale, they were 75 percent off! You gonna beat that?

Tell me about your mustache.
When my son was very small, he used to tease my daughter by saying, "I remember when Daddy had a beard." My daughter begged me to grow it back. So I did, and now I'm stuck with it, much to her regret. I use the wax 'cause it's wiry. I always think, When I die, they'll lay me out in a casket, and who's going to do my mustache?

What kind of lawyer are you?
God blessed me with a golden brain. To my knowledge, I am the only person who has worked both as a special prosecutor and a defense attorney at the same time.

Do you find that a suit makes you a better attorney?
If you pay attention to detail in your personal appearance, then your clients feel that you're paying attention to detail in a case. I once found a knife behind a toilet bowl that everyone else had missed. See what I mean?

GLORIA WARD
Beautician

What do you do?
I style hair and do all kinds of pretty things. I used to play drums in my husband's band.

What band was that?
A famous group called the Ink Spots. A song called "If I Didn't Care" made them very famous in 1939. My husband joined the band in the forties.

Were you always a drummer?
My husband taught me! We met at a concert years ago at the Theresa Hotel. He asked me if I do any typing. I do very little typing, but I said, "Oh, yes, I do typing."

How do you describe your style?
I may be a little flashy today with this short skirt, but basically I'm a conservative dresser. I love blazers. And I usually wear long braids, but I just got this wild hairstyle. It's actually a wig! I bought it at Mona wig shop, right here in Harlem. I love it. But it's getting too hot.

How about the rest of your makeup?
I've been doing the same thing since I was 25 years old. It's false eyelashes, and then I line it and then two or three layers of mascara on the lower lash. I don't know why! I just like it.

Is that a thumb ring?
It's actually my wedding band, but it's too big. And it turns out I like a thumb ring.

Do you live in Harlem?
No, I live in midtown, but my salon is up here. There's a lot of new stores coming to the area, and restaurants. Business is a little better, but not much.

What's the most popular hairstyle at your salon?
Locks. Seems like everybody wants the dreadlocks, and about fifteen years ago, I took a little course on them.

VINCENT OSHIN
Shop Manager and Stylist

What's your style?
It's not like I spend hours in front of the mirror going, "Oh, is this going to work? Blah blah blah." It's just what makes me feel comfortable, and it comes off like a practiced look, but it's not.

How long have you been in the U.S.?
I grew up in South London, East London, West London. I have been in New York since 2000, and I haven't looked back. I live in Prospect Heights, and it is peaceful, quiet, cheap, and nice. I love it.

Tell me about this outfit.
My wife made the hat. It's a line called Cora, and it's going to be debuting in January, so this hat is actually a sample. The coat is from a French vintage shop down on Brick Lane in London, and the scarf my missus brought back from India. I have on Helmut Lang trousers, I believe, and Nike trainers from Clientele, which is a premier sneaker shop.

Are you one of those sneaker fanatics?
No, no, no, no, no, no, no. If I like something, it might not be hip to someone else.

Do you have a favorite designer?
Helmut Lang's my favorite. He understood the man's form, you know? When you have it on, you just know that you smell of class.

Is that who influences your styling?
No. My major influence is my wife, because she is very passionate about what she does.

Your anniversary is coming up. Where are you going to go?
La Esquina, I guess. It's a place I said I'd never go to, but each time I've been there, it's really good.

SHELLEY HENNIG
Model/Actor

What do you do?

I'm a model-slash-actor. And I was Miss Teen USA in 2004.

Were you a pageant girl?

No, not at all. I was a dancer, and still am. I figured that entering the Miss Teen Louisiana pageant could get me to New York one day, and what do you know? Here I am. In New York.

Did you have pageant-girl style?

I went for a more simple look. It was kind of an experiment to see if I could do it at my comfort level and still win, so I designed my dress myself. It was white jersey and long, with just a little bow underneath the chest and crystal beading on the back. I wore my hair slicked back in a ponytail, and way less makeup than the other girls—who did look beautiful, I should say, but I felt beautiful being more natural.

Was it fun being Miss Teen USA?

Well, it got me where I am today! And Donald Trump was my boss for a year. Mr. Trump is a really good guy, but it was a long year. I was commuting and traveling around the world, but also I was a senior in high school in Louisiana.

Did you have a platform?

My brother passed away five years ago in a drunk-driving accident. As Miss Teen USA, your platform already has to do with teenage drinking, drugs, and violence, and I mainly spoke against drinking and driving. And I still work with Buzz Free Proms. It's this thing where you pledge not to drink at prom and all this great stuff. It's fun.

Tell me about your style.

It's so random! My stylist, Billy, taught me things, like that West Eighth Street is the unofficial shoe district of New York. That's where I got these boots. She also taught me that matching is not your No. 1 priority.

So what is?

Comfort. And of course you want to look good.

What are you doing today?

My dad's visiting, and he loves boats. So we're going to South Street Seaport because it's so beautiful. And my dad is seriously, like, my best friend. He's like a stand-up comedian at heart, and he doesn't even know it.

TERRY "COYOTE" MURPHY
Park Ranger

Do you always go shirtless?
Quite a bit. Whenever the weather's
right for it. There are some windy areas
downtown where it gets cold, but in
certain areas, the sun is magnified by all
the cement.

When did you start?
I've been doing it for twenty years. I used
to go over to the West Side. Some people
take everything off on the West Side,
on the old piers—especially during the
eighties they did. Quite a few people used
to ride bicycles with their shirts off in the
eighties, too, but that's not that common
anymore.

What do you do?
I'm a park ranger upstate, up in Orange
County, New York, and I do building
maintenance in Manhattan. And I guess
you could say that I do some acting
because I was in a film that went to
Sundance once. It was called *Native
American in Manhattan*.

Are you Native American?
I'm part Cherokee and part Irish. I was
also in *Native American in Manhattan*,
the sequel, by the way.

BRIAN SULLIVAN
Stay-at-Home Dad, with Saoirse

What are you guys doing today?
We dropped off my other daughter, Íte, who's 9, at her school, which is P.S. 41, and then walked over here. I'm the primary caretaker. Bleecker Street Park is the perfect place to while away the morning.

Your daughters have such unusual names.
Well, I've got a lot of Irish literature. Saoirse is an Irish name that roughly translates to "freedom." We like the sound of it, *Sur-sha*, but she may kill us for the spelling one day.

How would you describe your look?
My wife is in the fashion business, but my style is a mix of over-the-hill hipster and midlife crisis.

Does Saoirse pick out her own outfits?
She's only 3, but she insists on dressing herself. I only force the issue if it's about comfort, but even then we try to let her do what she wants. If she wants to wear a dress in nippy weather, we put pants on underneath.

Do you enjoy being a stay-at-home dad?
We went back and forth for a while—I worked in museums and Kelley, my wife, was at home—but I've done the lion's share. It's the hardest job I've ever had. I have a huge amount of respect for people who take the chance of not having a career. I'm an artist, and I teach sculpture at SVA in the evenings, but even if I had a high-paying job, I would feel ill at ease getting a nanny.

Are you friends with other caretaker dads?
When I first started, I felt like I was getting lots of stares from nannies and mothers alike. Now I walk down our block in Brooklyn and there's five guys pushing a stroller, so I'm no longer the odd man out.

Any plans for Father's Day?
We're going to celebrate early because Kelley has an intensive bookmaking class that weekend. We're thinking about doing a children's book together. I'm going to be pampered—get breakfast in bed and just lay around. I like to read. I'm a fairly big collector of books—I might not have as many if I actually had time to read them.

CLAUDIO DI BLASI AND ILARIA CASTELLI
Business Student and Fashion Showroom Assistant

How did you meet?

CLAUDIO: That's a good memory. We met each other in the Marais in Paris. A friend of us introduced each other, and it was love. Not really right away. We started going out together, then I had to go back to Italy to solve some issues. But we kept calling each other, and after two or three months, I met her again. I decided to move here because I wanted to go to business school. It was a little more difficult for her because she had a good job in a fashion showroom, but she was very brave.

Ilaria, what attracted you to Claudio?

ILARIA: His glamour, gentleman manner, and his eyes.

How would you describe your style?

ILARIA: I like to look fashionable and cool. And, of course, to be comfortable. This coat is Fay—I bought it in Milan.

CLAUDIO: I love clothes. That's why I am Italian, probably! These sunglasses are the classic aviator by Ray-Ban, and I am wearing Dandop jeans. You don't have them here, and I am sorry for you.

How would you describe each other's style?

CLAUDIO: Ilaria's style is pretty much like mine. That's why we are together. I love it when she wears Marni, and she loves Marni. The last thing I bought her was a Marc Jacobs skirt. We live across the street from the store, so I don't have to walk.

What's your favorite city to live in?

ILARIA: Paris. It's the city of love.

How did you feel about the pope's death?

CLAUDIO: I have a special feeling with what happened because I was in Vatican City for five years. I knew the pope. He was the spiritual dean at my university. I wanted to go to Rome and be there for the funeral, but I wasn't able to do it, so I went to St. Patrick's, and I followed everything on CNN.

Did you know him personally?

CLAUDIO: Not one-on-one, but we were together in groups. One thing I can tell you about is the look he used to give me. He looked me right in the eyes, like he was trying to transmit a message.

ROD RAYSON
Hairdresser

GINA CHU
Investor/Philanthropist

SOLA AGBAJE
Case Manager

GLENN STALEY AND KYLE MINGO
Party Promoters

How do you describe your style?
STALEY: Urban B-boy, like in the eighties.

MINGO: It's like a B-boy skater. I used to dress hip-hop style, but to me that's not even style, really. It's just watching the music videos and wearing what the rappers wear.

Where did you get these outfits?
STALEY: The clothing is from Pharrell, the rapper. He has a brand called Ice Cream, and I got it at Union in Soho. And the sneakers are from the Michael K. store; that's in Soho also. The bandanna is from Louis Vuitton.

MINGO: The shirt I'm wearing I got from my job at Brooklyn Industries. It's inspired by a Muslim who's looking for a kind of salvation because his family is poor. And then they're regular Levi's—I like hard denim, not too baggy—and sneakers from Kidrobot. I've got about 35 pairs of sneakers. The sunglasses I get from this guy at a flea market in Soho.

What's up with the neck scarves?
MINGO: I've been wearing the Afghanistan ones that they wear in, like, Iraq for a while. I saw this movie from the eighties called *Breakin'*, and I got inspired from that, like Kid 'n' Play and stuff. But those Afghanistan scarves are kind of hot, so I'm just taking it to the next level.

Why do you leave the size sticker on your hat?
STALEY: Some people do that to show how new it is, but then they wear the hat every day. When we do it, it's just to show that I don't wear it every day. It's like I'm saying I have so many hats I don't even pay attention to whether the sticker's still on there.

Where did you get your fronts done?
STALEY: Right here, at the Fulton Mall, by a guy named Yuri. A lot of guys like fronts on all their teeth, but I'm proud of my teeth, so I didn't want them all covered up.

What kind of parties do you promote?
MINGO: Dance-hall and reggae parties in Brooklyn. We're looking to do some in Soho, too.

Is Brooklyn style different from Manhattan?
MINGO: Sometimes I feel like we don't even belong here. People always stare at us like, What are they? Why do they look like that? But it's originality. We look more like guys who belong in Manhattan.

**Is Brooklyn style
different from Manhattan?**

Sometimes I feel like
we don't even belong here.
We look more like guys who
belong in Manhattan.

KOSUKE OKAWA
Student

What brought you to New York?

FIT. I wanted to study fashion, so I came three years ago. I enjoy New York, but in Japan everything makes sense more. Here is more exciting, with all the drama and the troubles.

The drama?

Yes! I'm writing a book right now because I've had so much drama. My apartment caught fire in Queens, and somebody broke into my other apartment and robbed me. Also, I got robbed in the elevator with a huge knife. And one of my roommates went really crazy mentally, and I had to put him in jail.

That's a lot of drama.

Yes! And I couldn't even get here. Last time I came, I flew fifteen hours to Detroit and I had all of my papers and everything and they still sent me home. Then I got in a huge car crash and broke my collarbone.

And you still wanted to come here?

Yeah. New York is very popular in Japan right now. That's why I'm writing so fast.

How do you get your hair like that?

My hairstylist gives me a permanent curl—it takes six hours, and my hair is so straight we have to do it twice. Luckily, she just moved to New York. She was No. 1 on the west coast of Japan, but she can't really speak English, so now she's a stylist at Q Hair on Bleecker Street. We're waiting for new chemicals to come from Japan— usually, I have a big, round Afro, bigger than Foxy Brown.

Do you shop a lot?

I go shopping every day. Whenever I go and find something special, I have to get it right away, because I don't want to think somebody else is wearing what I want. Sometimes I get five jackets in a day.

Where did you find this outfit?

I think the orange coat is vintage. I bought it in New York. I know that the pants are Alice + Olivia.

What is your style?

Kooan.

What does that mean?

It means Kooan. It's my nickname. I'm my style.

MARCELLA BELLE LUISO
Senior Consultant,
The Daniels Company

What are you wearing?
An Adele Ross. She was a high-society Madison Avenue designer back in the Kennedy years. She was very glamorous, this woman. She looked like Jean Harlow. I bought the collection from her niece. It turns out that I'd had an Adele Ross years ago that I wore to a party for an Italian furrier. There I was, competing with Sophia Loren's agent's daughter, so I really needed an exclusive gown. And now, many moons later, Adele is back in my life!

And the accessories?
My little bag is vintage from Florence, my jewels are from an Arizona designer called Jean Stetson. The shoes I'm wearing are from Tanino Crisci, one of the most elite Italian designers.

How long have you been coming to the opera?
My parents loved opera very, very, very much. Since I was three years old I heard it on the record player day and night. I also do volunteer work at the New Rochelle Opera.

What did you do to get ready for the evening?
I got my hair done by a very lovely lady. She's quite excellent, I think. The name of the company is Gil Ferrer, and they're located on East 74th Street. My exceptional hairdresser is called Paige.

How would you describe your look tonight?
Classic, because truly beautiful clothing is classic. This fabric would probably cost $500 a yard these days. To me, fashion is an art form, just like opera.

What are you wearing?
An Adele Ross.
She was a high-society
Madison Avenue designer
back in the Kennedy
years. She looked like
Jean Harlow.

NILS ASMUSSEN
Tourist

What are you doing today?
I am waiting for the Heartland Brewery to open. I am bringing my girlfriend lots of American beer when I go home.

Do you get lost much?
Yes and no. Usually, I want to go to a place, but on my way I see something interesting. Then I go to visit this new place. And I never regret it. But the subway system is confusing. The subway does not stop at every station. I would suggest more subway maps at the subway station and also more public street maps in lower Manhattan. There is no easy system there with avenues and streets.

BRIDGID RYAN
Translator/Chaperone

What are you doing today?
I'm taking twenty Japanese kids to Soho. I'm a translator. It's basically like Camp America, and I'm in charge.

How did you learn Japanese?
I like to talk so much that I decided I'd learn another language, and I lived in Tokyo for four months. It's very useful knowing Japanese. It makes me realize what makes me me.

Where are you from?
Philadelphia, but I'm trying to get a job in New York. I'm reading *Breakfast at Tiffany's*. A good friend has offered to take me all around the villages or boroughs or whatever you call them because I have this dream of finding an apartment with the sun coming in where I can grow plants. And then I'll get my library card and go to the grocery store.

SAM PARKER
Art Student

Where are you going today?
To have lunch with my girlfriend. She always likes it when I'm better dressed than she is. I made a New Year's resolution to try to wear a tie every single day, and it's been going pretty well.

Have you broken it yet?
If I round up, then no.

How long does it take you to get dressed in the morning?
I plan my outfits out in advance. I lay in bed and think about my colors: Tomorrow, how about white on top, black on bottom, gray in the middle? Like that. It's really just twenty minutes or so to pick out the pieces in the morning. And I just mess up my hair, because I like rough hair and clean clothes. Have the mind crazy but the body tight.

Is that your fashion advice?
No. My advice is, dress to undress, if you know what I mean.

Where do you shop?
Yves Saint Laurent has the best textiles I've seen recently, so for pieces like ties and pocket squares and ascots, I go there. I also like Opening Ceremony. Jeffrey is probably my favorite store in the world. I have a little bit of a problem at Jeffrey. It's very hard for me to go in and not buy something. And Thom Browne I love, too.

You have expensive taste for a student.
I have help. My mother understands and sympathizes. I got an internship at Opening Ceremony. I figure that if I go work in fashion, I'll get free clothes or just spend all of my money on clothes. It will be a nice little circle.

What's the last thing you bought?
A tailored shirt from Freemans Sporting Club. It's got an outdoorsman quality, but it's hand-tailored at the same time. I think that's a nice relationship. It's really masculine, you know?

Do you have style icons?
Yes. How about Buster Keaton, Marcello Mastroianni, and Thelonious Monk? I like them all so much. Not specifically for their style, but they all have a good sense of humor.

Do you?
Yes.

Tell me a joke.
No.

**KELLY MCGRAW, NICOLE GARRISON,
DANA GREENAWALD, AND
DANIELLE WILKINSON**
Aspiring Models

DUANE LITTLES
Actor

What are you wearing today?

My sneakers are from Shoe Mania on 14th Street. The leather outfit is something I got from H&M about three years ago. I used to work there, so I could see things before they came in and snatch them when they hit the floor. This outfit was actually in the young girls' department, but it works! The blazer was a gift from my girlfriend; I think she bought it at Macy's. I found my hat in that little market down by Tower Records on Broadway.

How much hair is under there?

It's to the middle of my back. I started growing it in the fall of '95. It was never really a conscious decision; my hair just started getting a little wild, and the next thing you know, I started growing out the top of my dreads. Around the fall of '97, I decided to let the whole thing grow and become a part of me. Not a fashion statement—part of my personality.

Is it hard to take care of?

Sometimes I get it done professionally. I went to a place called Locks-n-Chop on 34th Street for a while, but then I started to go to a friend of mine who's also in the entertainment business. But mostly I just take care of it myself. I clean it with witch hazel—I use a Q-tip for my scalp and a cotton swab for the rest of my head. And I oil it. Right now I'm using a really good oil called Luster's Pink Plus. You can get it at Duane Reade.

So you're an actor. What kind of roles do you play?

I've been on *Chappelle's Show* twice. In the latest episode, I play a barber. The first time, I did a sketch called "Odweeds" about a fake marijuana product. A lot of people have seen it—I get stopped on the street. But I also design clothes.

Like what?

I buy stuff and retool it. I'll add buttons, paint, pieces of denim. I was doing trucker hats for a while, and then women's handbags. Now I'm coming into a T-shirt phase.

Trucker hats? Aren't you over trucker hats?

I don't wear them anymore. Not because other people don't—I just don't feel the need. I've gone through that phase. It was totally a fad. In the beginning, you don't know that, but then pretty soon you can tell.

What are you doing today?
Well, I just finished giving a speech at the Pierre Hotel about abortion rights. I used to be the chairman of NARAL. And now I'm heading home. I live at the River House. We're having Andrew Cuomo for cocktails tonight. No, not Andrew, Mario. The former governor.

Were you at NARAL a long time?
A while. I'm 82 now. I was ambassador to Norway at one point, and I worked for the New York Stock Exchange. I still sit on the board of the U.S.-Japan Foundation, which I co-founded, and a couple other organizations as well. And I'm very politically active for the Democrats.

What do you think of Samuel Alito?
He seems to be a chap with a good deal of experience. Looks very well qualified. Too conservative, but I would imagine he'll get through. I felt sorry for the other one, that poor lady. They really went after her like attack dogs.

Did you like Norway?
I loved it. I like the Scandinavians—they're good people. And I do like to ski. My husband, Angier Biddle Duke, was also an ambassador—to Morocco, Denmark, Spain . . .

How would you describe your style?
Very classic. Obviously. Now, let's get on with it.

Were there certain wardrobe pressures as an ambassador?
I've never been self-conscious about my style. I dress the way I dress, and if it doesn't suit the job, that's too bad. I dress conservatively, I suppose, but I'm 82! My favorite designer was Geoffrey Beene, who is, I'm sad to say, gone. You know, I was a fashion editor once! On the *New York Journal-American*, which is also long gone. I'm like the cat that keeps coming back.

Is this outfit Geoffrey Beene?
It's always Geoffrey Beene. He was a great cutter, sort of like Balenciaga.

What was your favorite career?
Working for the *Journal-American* when La Guardia was mayor. What a delight he was! Bloomberg has some of the same personality, you know. But I really loved La Guardia. I was one of the lone women wandering around, and I guess if you're a young, pretty blonde girl, that helps, but he was so nice to me.

JULIA DONALDSON
Student

What came first, the hair or the gloves?
The hair. I love to change my hair color.
And then when I found the gloves at
Arden B., I just thought they were perfect.

How many colors has it been?
It's been flame-colored, it's been pink
and purple. My normal hair is so boring.
I really like the costume element of
dressing. I really like how you can be
different characters all at once. In this
outfit I'm like Alice in Wonderland
meets some old spidery widow. I get very
different reactions with the different
outfits, but in New York, it's much better
than in North Carolina, where I'm from.
Here, people seem to find it fun and
refreshing and they enjoy it, whereas in
Raleigh, I'm just looked at as bizarre.

Why did you move to New York?
I've always wanted to move here ever since
I was little. And now I'm in my foundation
year at Parsons. I'm going to go into
fashion.

**Has the city lived up to your
expectations?**
It's perfect. Maybe there will be things I
get tired of in a few years, but at this point,
I'm not tired of anything at all. I like to
walk down St. Marks because there's lots
of bright wigs. And I love Ricky's—they
have great eyelashes.

Who are your favorite designers?
I really love Elsa Schiaparelli because I
think she took crazy costume elements
and made them into fashion. I think it's
amazing that there was Coco Chanel
doing suits, and Elsa Schiaparelli doing
Medusa-inspired hat-things. I like
Olivier Theyskens and what he's doing for
Rochas. It's like a darker personality for
the whole ladylike thing.

So what hair color is next?
Well, I have to bleach my hair before I dye
it, and it's bad for it. I really have to control
myself sometimes. I'm waiting until it
gains strength, and then it's going to be
light pink with black on the ends. When
I think about Valentine's Day colors and
all of the stores rolling out their valentine
displays, the combination of pink and
black really interests me.

DONALD ABRAMS
Legal Secretary

Where are you from?
New York, born and bred. I'm from the Bronx, which I call the Big B—not Brooklyn. That's the small B.

Where'd you get the suit?
The labels are cut out of the jacket because I bought it at Daffy's. But if you check in the pants, it does say Hugo Boss. I couldn't believe it when I saw that.

And that Louis Vuitton portfolio!
That's my favorite. That was a gift to me from my significant other, I must say. His name is Brian, and he got it through eluxury.com.

And the shoes?
Stacy Adams, I believe. I bought them out of Florsheim.

Is that a key or a ring you're wearing?
It's a key chain, but I wear it as jewelry, believe it or not. It's such an eye-pleaser. My whole thing is that it's the key to my heart. It's sterling silver and I bought it at a flea market. The secret is that it's also a bottle opener, but no one can tell.

How'd you get so into fashion?
My grandmother, God rest her soul, she was a senior pattern-maker. I used to sit in the house and watch her make patterns from brown paper bags. I was her muse, I guess you could say. And my aunt, she worked at Macy's for twenty years.

Is there someone whose style you admire?
I used to admire the attorneys; I like a very starched, professional look. I've been doing this for twenty years, it's got to rub off.

Any special grooming rituals?
I normally don't tell my little secrets. I have one barber, who I pray to. His name is Shamel, and he's at Swirl & Curls Design in Parkchester. It's a unisex type of place.

Do you think Martha deserves to be in jail?
I love Martha Stewart. There are a whole lot of people out there who deserve to be in jail much more than she does.

Who would you put on the Supreme Court?
I would have to say Colin Powell. I don't know why, I could just see him in those robes sitting on the bench. He would look amazing.

VONN JACKSON
Phone Operator

How do you describe your style?
I'm trendy, I think, but I don't like to wear what everyone else has. I try to go left if everyone else goes right, you know?

Where did you get this outfit?
The sandals are that whole Roman thing, but somehow when I wear them with the hat, they take on a cowgirl effect. I got the dress from Strawberry's and the hat at Target, but we call it "Tarjay" where I come from.

Where do you come from?
East New York. It's Brooklyn, but it's more like Queens, except that it's not Queens.

Whose style do you admire?
Gwen Stefani. Whoever her stylist is, I love you.

What kind of singer are you?
I have songs up on MySpace. I would say it's R&B—if I had to compare myself to anyone, it would be a mix between Brandy and Aaliyah. I'm soft and sultry.

What about the swimsuit modeling?
How many times can you take a picture in a swimsuit and not get bored? I like doing stuff better. I used to do music videos and extra parts in movies.

Any summer plans?
The beach is cool. I usually try to go somewhere different every year. I went to Puerto Rico this year; last year it was Jamaica and the Bahamas. Other than that, I'm just going to eat barbecue, party a bit, and pay the bills.

What do you do?
My real job is as a phone operator for Kaplan Test Prep. But I'm also a singer and aspiring songwriter. And a swimsuit model. That's about it. Oh, I'm in school, too.

JOSHUA KU
Student and Model

How did you get into modeling?
I worked at Starbucks for a while, and another guy there used to be a model, sort of. He told me I should try out. The first agency I went to was called ReQuest, and they just picked me up, I guess.

Do you like it?
Well, sometimes it requires you to do things that you would only do in your bathroom by yourself. Which is not hard, it's just something to get used to. For me, right now it's the right idea. I'm sorry, I can be really abstract sometimes.

What do you mean?
Well, I'm more of a student than a model. I like it for the traveling and stuff. I did this shoot for *L'Uomo Vogue* that was probably the biggest thing I've done. They didn't pay me at all because they said it's more helpful for me than for anyone else, I guess. They said that was their "payment."

What do you study?
I go to Baruch, and I'm undeclared. Maybe I'll do advertising or something.

When did you dye your hair?
That was for a magazine called *Pop* in London. It was sort of a Japanese-inspired editorial.

Do you like it?
I think it makes me look intimidating and unapproachable. It seems like it's a given that having this hair makes me some kind of an asshole—or maybe just an outcast. My friends say it makes me look better.

How do you describe your style?
I just go to H&M. I try to be simple because there are a lot of things to worry about other than clothing. Like work. Relationships. School. But everyone's vain to a certain degree, so I guess it's really about being as simple and comfortable as possible, but at the same time looking all right.

FREDERICA MONACO
Mother

What are you doing today?
This is my shopping day. I went to Bergdorf Goodman, Henri Bendel, and Saks. I love department stores. It's easy to return something if I change my mind.

Do you often change your mind?
My style is very classic. I bought a trench coat the other day in a new color for me—lime green. The cut was very good, but I wore it once and decided that I hated it, so I returned it. I like beige.

Tell me about this outfit.
It's a shearling coat from Joseph, and of course I have my great big Birkin bag. It was a present from my husband five years ago when our son was born. I'm French, so I've got some connections at Hermès. We didn't have to be on the wait list.

How long have you been in America?
Eleven years. I came here to go to Amherst College, and then I worked for the French consulate. I had lots and lots of parties to go to, and I could only wear French clothing. So after I stopped working, I went straight to Ralph Lauren. I love Ralph Lauren because you always know that five years from now, it's still going to look nice.

Has your style changed since moving here?
American women are much more sophisticated than French women because there is so much more choice. French women are very picky, and they don't spend so much money on clothing: They choose things that are going to last. And they're not getting their hair blow-dried and the manicure and pedicure every single week. They are less polished.

Is your husband French?
He's American—a real New Yorker. We met at Barneys. He thought I was a model. He gave me his card and asked if he could take my picture. Many people give me their cards and I throw them away, but this was different—he wasn't pushy. A few days later I called him and that was it. We never even took any pictures for a year.

Is he a photographer?
It's his passion. But he's in real estate.

Are you glad you married an American?
American men love to be a father. French men are so concerned with the way they look.

Is your husband French?
He's American—a real New Yorker. We met at Barneys. He thought I was a model. He gave me his card and asked if he could take my picture.

SHAKTI WESTROM
Jazz Archivist

Is Shakti your real name?
It was given to me when I was seventeen years old at an ashram in Virginia called Yogaville. The guru there gave it to me. He was the swami who presided over Woodstock, actually.

What does it mean?
It means "power-energy." It's a Sanskrit word. It's anything in the world you can touch.

What name did your parents give you?
Lauren. I don't make them say Shakti.

Do you teach yoga?
I don't right now. Right now I work as a curator and archivist for someone with a large jazz collection, and on the side I do lots of volunteer work. I volunteer at the Beth Israel Rape Crisis Center, and I volunteer for *Spread* magazine, which is the only American publication written by and for sex workers.

Are you a sex worker?
It's a policy that no one on staff has to answer that question if asked.

Tell me about your outfit.
It's my grandmother's leopard coat, and the dress is an old vintage Betsey Johnson, from the late eighties I think. My style is that I love pattern. Not small, busy pattern, bold pattern and color.

Do you teach yoga?
I don't right now. Right now I work as a curator and archivist for someone with a large jazz collection, and on the side I do lots of volunteer work.

Southampton
CASUALS

KAREEM DIMITRIOUS COLLIE AND DONALD "RAY" FRANKLIN II
Design Partners

You look so sharp.
KAREEM: We're heading to a presentation, so we want to look sharp. I'm doing my Professor Collie garb. We try to stay on top of our game. We're businessmen and we're icons for our business. It always helps to think of it holistically like that.

RAY: Kareem represents the creative and I represent the business side, and I think our style reflects that.

Tell me about these outfits.
KAREEM: These are herringbone slacks by Yoko Devereaux, paired with a nice cream turtleneck sweater. I was afraid of looking too Euro, so I put on this little straw hat that I usually wear in the summertime.

RAY: This is a blue Ralph Lauren blazer that I bought and then changed the buttons. They were gold with a sailor emblem, and now they're silver with crests. It's a Rod Keenan hat—rabbit fur with an alligator strap—a Paul Smith scarf, a Bruno Cucinelli sweater, and an Armani watch.

Do your looks help your business?
KAREEM: I had a client walk into a meeting one day and say to me, if you had come in here dressed any other way, I would ask to see your portfolio, but I can tell by the way that you're dressed that you're sharp and that you're on it. Let's just do it.

RAY: When people meet us for the first time, before we even open our mouths, they get excited. They want to work with us. It's a certain atmosphere that we bring, a certain aura.

DAMIEN KLOSOWSKI
Commercial Real Estate Agent

What's up with your eyes?

People say I look like Lestat, but I'd like to look even more like a vampire. I don't need to jump out from behind corners and scream or anything. I just wait for people to see my eyes.

ALEXANDRA PEREZ
Expediter

What do you do?

Oh, god. Do you really want to know?
We get permits, we deal with permits. It's
growing on me, but it's a job, not a career.
I love fashion, and I want to get into that.

What do you want to do in fashion?

I'm a weird person 'cause I say "fashion,"
but I can't look at a fabric and say what it
is or anything like that. I just know when
I see something if I like it or not, and I
always get a reaction from other people.
So I think I could do consulting, like if
someone came into a specific retail store
I could dress them. I'm in love with the
show *What Not To Wear*. I'm totally stuck
on it. I don't even care if it's a repeat, I'll
watch anyway.

What makes you like something?

I need something to pop. And for me,
pretty much 99% of the time, it's the
shoes. Every week I get a pair of shoes. I
counted last year and I had eighty pairs of
closed-toe shoes. I didn't count my sandals
or my boots. You can imagine how crazy
it makes my boyfriend, and I'm just like,
shut up. You don't understand.

When do you not like something?

My pet peeve is when I see people who are
wearing clothes that are not in season. I
know, I know, it gets warm sometimes,
but you're gonna wear capris and sneakers
with scarves and hats and gloves? It kills
me. I'm like, what are you doing? One half
of your body is one season, and the other
half is another!

Does your boyfriend like fashion, too?

He's a loss-prevention manager at
the Donna Karan store, so he has
discounts, which I use sometimes but
most of the things they have there I
could find somewhere else for cheaper.
I love a bargain.

Where do you buy shoes?

I'll go anywhere from Payless to Aldo—
like these shoes are from Aldo—to BCBG.
Clothes I could do without, but shoes, no
way. . . . Stilettos especially.

PAR PAREKH
Filmmaker

Tell me about your style.
Really? But there's so much else to talk about.

What would you rather talk about?
Ahmadinejad.

What about him?
He's a madman.

ALAN M. ADES
Advisory Director to the Met

Do you always wear white-tie?
No, but we're having dinner at the Met Opera Club. I thought, I haven't worn my white-tie outfit in a while.

ANTONIA NIECKE
Tourist

What are you doing today?
Just sightseeing with my soccer club.
We've been traveling around the U.S.,
playing soccer against the town clubs in
Roanoke and Camden.

How did you do?
We mostly won all of the games. I wouldn't
say we were better than the Americans,
because I have not played against every
American, but it could be. We were
definitely a little bit better, at least.

Where did you get the rabbit ears?
Over by the harbor before we took the boat
to Ellis Island. I realized that I could be a
Playboy Bunny for Halloween, and also
that they are just kind of funny.

What do you think of New York?
It is a little bit big and crazy. You can cross
the street and find a totally different city.
Here you have a homeless person sleeping
on a bench, and then you turn a corner
and there are very expensive shops.

DERICK, INGRID, M. ALEXANDRA, AND ELIZABETH ANNE GEORGE

Anesthesiologist, Stay-at-Home Mom, and Child Prodigies

What are you doing today?

INGRID: We started our day with lunch at Jojo and then walked over to Barneys. Derick got a full Brioni outfit. We also went to Teuscher Chocolates, which we love, and then we went up to Robert Marc for glasses. We'll end the day at Café Gray. The girls have a piano recital tomorrow, so it's a bit of a fun day. They've been musical since the age of 3. They play unbelievably difficult, impossible things.

Where did these outfits come from?

INGRID: My dress is from Barneys, and the girls' dresses are Laura Biagiotti from Zitomer.

DERICK: My jacket is Zegna.

Do you always dress up for a family afternoon?

INGRID: We are beautiful people inside and out. I start with the outside so when someone sees us, it's a pleasant experience. And then when they get to know us, we are lovely people inside.

DERICK: When I was in high school, I was voted best-dressed and most likely to succeed. They call me GQ at work. Even in scrubs, I look good. When you're in anesthesia, you have five to ten minutes to convince people that you're not the last person they're ever going to see. If you present yourself well, it gives the patient confidence.

What are your plans for the summer?

M. ALEXANDRA: I'm going to Johns Hopkins' camp for advanced kids in Saratoga and doing physics. And in the fall I'll be going to St. Paul's School. There's no dress code!

ELIZABETH ANNE: I'm also going to Johns Hopkins' camp, but for math.

INGRID: They had to place three grades higher than their own grade level to get in. Alexandra got 1300 on the SATs at the age of 12.

What's wrong with you? Anything?

INGRID: To those whom much is given, much is expected. And we've been given a lot. Right now we're listening to *Creating Affluence* by Deepak Chopra, and following the A-to-Z principles of attitude. A is for all possibilities, B is for better than your best, and L is for love. Love everyone. We believe that, and we try to live that every day.

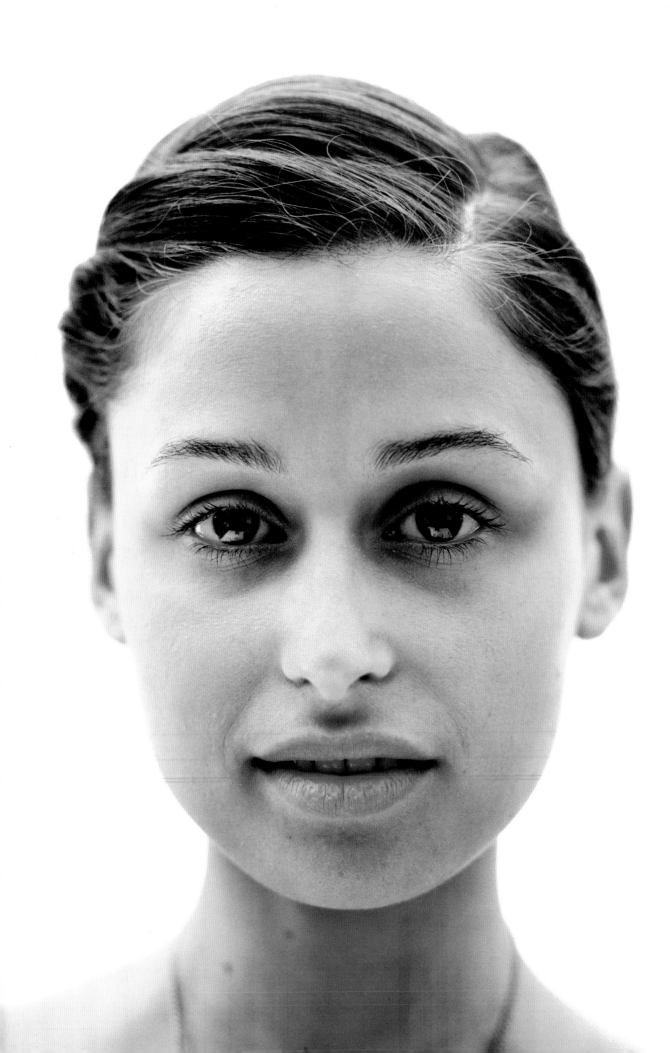

LISA MAYOCK
Fashion Designer

What do you do?
I'm one half of the clothing label Vena Cava. Sophie and I have been designing together for about three years, since we went to Parsons.

What's your style like?
I love pairing things that are throwaway with things that are really memorable. I design the same way.

Do you have style icons?
Oh, yes. Hunter S. Thompson. I can't think of anyone else who looked so good in short shorts and jogging shoes. My favorite thing in the world is when people can pull off really nerdy looks.

Fashion Week's coming up. What's your new collection like?
I'm really inspired by this idea of Japonisme. It's French and European designers who were influenced by Japan when trade opened up in the nineteenth century.

Tell me about this outfit.
The dress is from an old Vena Cava pattern. Then I'm wearing my leggings, because I went to yoga class this morning. The necklace was my great-aunt's safety pin with pearls on it that I just threw onto a chain. The ring I got yesterday in the West Village. I tried it on and couldn't get it off, so I had to buy it.

Where did you get your shoes?
Some tiny thrift shop. They're little-old-lady orthopedics. I have a really romantic idea of dressing myself when I get old. I'm going to wear a turban and gold-lamé pants and be really eccentric. I can't wait.

MCCLOUD ZICMUSE
Aesthete

What do you do?
I'm an artist, musician, and letterpress
printer. I press ephemera, business cards,
posters, record covers, invitations. And I
sing French children's songs. The name of
my band is Le Ton Mité, which means "the
moth-eaten tone."

Do you play for children?
No, mainly for adults. I'm playing the
Bowery Ballroom in January. I sing songs
about, like, a really nice summer when
I swam in phosphorescent water and
walked around the dunes.

Why do you sing in French?
Because of my fascination with French
culture. Spending time in Canada got
me started. I was finally invited to play
in a festival in France, so I see what I'm
doing as developing a cross-continental
relationship.

**Do you always wear such
bright colors?**
I used to live in Olympia, Washington.
And when there's clouds in the sky all the
time, you learn how to be your own sun, to
emit energy and light. I find color to be the
most satisfying thing on earth. Not better
than sex, but a great complement.

Do you have a favorite color?
Orange, yellow, baby blue, and a green
that's a little darker than chartreuse:
95 percent yellow, 4 percent blue, and 1
percent black.

Are you synaesthetic?
To a certain degree, but it's more
emotional. It crosses into the realm of the
psyche rather than taste or hearing. I find
that there's a lot of sharing between the
visual and the songs that I write.

You must have loved *The Gates*.
It was pretty good. I'm glad that Christo
can make a living doing that. I'm glad he's
not on the street or something. But I don't
feel a strong bond. It's more like a visual
high five.

Do you always wear such bright colors?
I find color to be the most satisfying thing on earth. Not better than sex, but a great complement.

JASMINE GOLESTANEH
Musician

What kind of music do you make?
I'm in a band called Seasick. The name just kind of came to me in the middle of the night once. We play dark, experimental, psychedelic folk-rock. I sing, I play guitar, I write all the songs. It's sort of my band.

How would you describe your style?
As a semi-catastrophic accident. It's an improvised thing. I'm very attracted to color and to form, but I don't think about it in terms of fashion. I just sort of end up wearing something.

Where do you buy clothes?
I'll find things in the street, or they'll find me. I have a bizarre relationship with clothes. It's like they're lively creatures that wind up on my body. Like this dress: I found it at a thrift shop, and it totally stood out from across the room—like, "You are the one."

How do you dress when you perform?
If there's a visual counterpart to the sound, I dress like that. I like to make it a bit theatrical and fantastical and eccentric and out-of-the-ordinary, but not like a costume for the sake of wearing a costume. As a performer, wearing something wacko can bring out different parts of your personality.

Which part of your personality does red bring out?
Well, I just recorded a music video in this dress. Red is an angry-but-happy color.

How long have you been in New York?
Two and a half years. I was living in London, and I had a dream that I should move here. Two weeks later, I was on a plane. I'd been in London about fifteen years, but as soon as I got here, I knew exactly why I came.

Why's that?
It's a very spiritual place, New York. There's such an instant karma— what you put in, you get out. I'm very multicultural—my mother's from Latvia, my father's from Iran, I was born in the U.S., and I grew up in England and France. Here, I feel normal.

Where do you buy clothes?
I'll find things in the street, or they'll find me. I have a bizarre relationship with clothes. It's like they're lively creatures that wind up on my body.

MAXIMILLIAN MEYER
Baby

BRIAN ERMANSKI
Resaler

What do you call that look?
It's Edwardian punk fop. I usually wear
the same outfit for a month. I'll go a week
without showering. I'm only on, like, day
two. This is my Prince of Elizabeth look,
which I'm wearing because I make art
outside an abandoned building on Prince
and Elizabeth. Today, Vito Schnabel
is coming to see it. He's, like, the best
gallerist in New York. He's going to pay
thousands of dollars for my work.

Is that how you make money?
I buy used clothes at thrift stores, and then
I resell them at expensive places like Ina
and Resurrection. I can find a seventies
Yves Saint Laurent men's suit for $10 in
a thrift store and then get $125 at Ina.
When I was a freshman at NYU, I got lots
of copies of *Wallpaper* and studied. I'm a
visual learner.

What's going on with your eye makeup?
I woke up and it was still on. I try to put
on a lot. It's a lived-in look. I like the fact
that it reminds me of the night before.

So what happened last night?
I don't remember. I live for today.
Not yesterday, not tomorrow. Wait—I
guess that goes against what I just said.
Dammit.

Do you have style icons?
I admire my friend Countess's style. She's
a real countess, from, like, London. She's
just London extravagant: eighties punk.
Very royal.

Are you into royal style?
When you invent something, you have
to live it. And I invented that I'm the
Prince of Elizabeth, so in that way, I like
royal style. I'm actually in love with the
Queen of Broome—she's a supermodel.
But sometimes I'll just wear long johns
for, like, three months. Everyone was like,
What are you doing? But then I saw long
johns in *V* magazine. Maybe they saw me,
or maybe they saw some other first ape.

What?
You don't know the first-ape theory? It's
that all the apes in the world think of
the same thing at the same time: like the
wheel, for example. And some apes put
the idea into production, so they get all the
credit. Like, Madonna has a boom box in
her new video. I've been carrying around
a boom box for four months. No, eleven.
I'm a first ape, but I never get things into
production. I'm going to be better about it
this year.

ALBERT WEST
Cowboy

KIM MAHNKE
Shopclerk

JIM AND BONNIE CROWN
Professor Emeritus and
Literary Agent

I love your berets.
JIM: We lived for a year in Paris, once.
They don't really wear them over there
anymore, I suppose, but they're nice for
here, for taking a walk, and we do like to
walk. There's a saying, I think it's French,
that you are what you eat, but I think that
you are what you see, so we like to wander.

Where do you wander?
JIM: We live on Tenth Street, and they've
really fixed up the West Side, so we go
out on the pier. You can see the Statue of
Liberty and a little bit of the Verrazano
Bridge, and of course there are a lot of
things to see as you go along.

**Have you lived on Tenth Street a
long time?**
JIM: Since the fifties. There's a Picasso
statue down by NYU, and you can see the
Chrysler Building from University Place.
It's generally pretty civilized down here.
There's some theater, and quite a range
of food.

Do you have children?
BONNIE: We don't, and that's by choice.
We do have some children we like to take
around. We like children, and people
always wonder how we get by without,
but we get the ones we want when we
want them.

Do you have berets in lots of colors?
BONNIE: Pink, yellow, brown, white . . .
they're just so easy to stuff in your pocket.

JIM: I like to think that I've pacified the
green beret.

Your life sounds so idyllic.
JIM: We do have a good life, but you know,
there's never enough time to do all the
things you want to do, and that includes
loafing around.

Do you have berets in lots of colors?

Pink, yellow, brown, white . . . they're just so easy to stuff in your pocket.

How would you describe your style?
Kind of modern, kind of old Jewish grandma. I love to wear grandma clothes really tight. Sexy grandma!

MIRIAM SIROTA
Real-Estate Broker

What are you wearing today?
The shoes are Miu Miu platform espadrilles that I bought at Beacon's Closet. I nearly fainted when I saw them. They were $50. The jacket and bag were made by a friend of mine, Judi Rosen. She owns a store called the Good, the Bad, and the Ugly on East Ninth Street.

What's in the bag?
Keys to every apartment in New York City because I'm a real-estate broker with Corcoran. And I usually have a hat thrown in there, just in case the moment calls out for a hat.

What kind of moment calls out for a hat?
If it rains. I'm not an umbrella chick.

Do you have a lot of beauty rituals?
I get extensions done at the Sally Hershberger salon by Ryan, and he's fantastic. I notice that a lot of young gals are very into their hair-removal routine. At a party recently I heard about one girl who gets waxed before she goes to the gynecologist. People think I'm high maintenance if I carry a parasol for the sun, but getting waxed for the gyno— that's high maintenance. My big thing is that the bush is back, and I don't mean the president.

Where do you live?
In Bed-Stuy. I just bought a house there, and it's beautiful. I love it because people really get dressed up out there, like for church.

How do you feel about gentrification?
Look, I work at the Corcoran Group. It's very difficult to talk about gentrification because even in the middle of Greenwich Village, you have people in the top 1 percent income bracket living beside people who are below the poverty line. It's not like Kansas City or Los Angeles, where there are people on the other side of the tracks.

Did you always want to sell real estate?
I wanted to be a magician, or an actress. I am also a singer.

What kind?
I sing to my clients. "Sunrise, Sunset." And I take requests. Sometimes we all sing together.

KEVIN TOWNLEY
Actor

What are you doing today?
I've been taking a screenwriting class with Michael Showalter. A friend and I were at Barnes & Noble doing some reading for it. It's a great class, but it's made me realize that screenwriting is a huge, stressful undertaking, not just something you do when you're not being cast. I think I'm going to just wait to be cast.

How's that going?
I just had a small part in *My Super Ex-Girlfriend.* I played Eddie Izzard's character in a high-school flashback. And I just finished a play, I'm in a band called Electric Fiction, and I perform with an improv group called Fancy Dragon.

Was *My Super Ex-Girlfriend* your first movie?
Yes. Ivan Reitman is still one of the great comedy directors. It was like going straight to Broadway.

How did you get into improv?
I remember seeing *Waiting for Guffman* and learning that the actors had only been given an outline. I was like, I could never do that. Except that maybe I could. I decided that it's my dream to be in a Christopher Guest film and I'd better be ready if it happens.

Tell me about your style.
I guess it's really Diane Keaton chic. When I saw *Annie Hall,* I was totally blown away, and I started dressing off-kilter right then. I decided to dress on the outside how I feel on the inside.

And how is that?
It's mostly about layers. I had one teacher who told me that real intelligence is finding connections between seemingly unrelated things. That's what I do with my layering.

Tell me about your style.

I guess it's really Diane Keaton chic.

TIM HORAN
Retiree

What are you doing today?
Walking the dog in the park before I go
out to play bridge.

Tell me about your style.
Everybody says I still dress the way I
dressed in high school. I grew up in
Cambridge, and Harvard's influence was
very strong. It was seersucker suits, white
bucks, all that.

I like your neck scarf.
I had neck surgery two and a half years
ago, and it still doesn't look like my neck
to me. Everyone says, "God, you're chic." I
say, "Kid, I just don't want to wear a tie."
I really don't have much of an ego about
what I wear. My granddaughter—who
is my life, by the way—just asked me if I
changed my glasses, and I said,
"Oh, did I?"

When did you come to New York?
December 1945. The day I got out of the
Army. I was in the OSS, which people in
Washington called "Oh So Social." I thank
God for it, because it really made my war.
If I'd been stuck in the infantry, I would've
been shot by my own men.

What did you do for work?
Well, I should've quit the goddamned
scene in New York and been a writer,
but as it was, I worked in advertising, I
worked at a magazine called *Coronet*, I
worked at Radio Free Europe, I worked
at Bantam Books. Basically, anything that
was guaranteed to not make me rich, I
accepted. It's the Irish curse. But I did win
a lot of money on television quiz shows.
They were all rigged in those days. I had to
miss questions to build up suspense. They
couldn't throw me off because I got a lot
of fan mail; nuns in Oregon were praying
for me.

Any summer plans?
We've had 16 years in Bridgehampton
in what was truly one of the best houses,
but we sold that because we spend the
summer in Italy and the winter in Florida.
The past seven years, we've been in Lucca,
but the villa is too big—30 rooms.

Do you shop in Italy?
Oh, yes. At Brioni.

RAVEN BURGOS
Writer

What do you do?
I just graduated from college. I used to run an online raw food magazine, and now I'm going to write about fashion online.

Are you a raw food-ist?
No. God, no. I like pork.

Tell me about your outfit.
The pants are from Chile—I just came back from living there for a while. The belt's from Guatemala and the ring's from India. It's my mom's ex-boyfriend's Harley-Davidson shirt that I cut up and sewed back together. When I go to different countries, I incorporate the jewelry from there. I'm multination; I'm bilingual.

Where are you from?
I was born in St. Vincent's Hospital, but I went to a Christian missionary school in Honduras: I'm Honduran. Now I live in Williamsburg. Everybody has their own ideas as to what ethnicity I am. People think a lot of different things, and the way that I dress totally changes that: Sometimes I'm rockabilly and I'll look one way, but then I'll go sort of Dolly Parton meets Hedi Slimane, with big bouffant hair and skinny, skinny suits.

Do you plan your outfits in advance?
I used to. Every time I came up with a decent outfit, I'd write it down. But I realized that it actually has everything to do with my mood, because I can wear the exact same thing and feel totally different. But the hair's always got to be big, big and huge.

What is your tattoo?
I got it about five years ago. It's from the Mayan ruins in Honduras. It's a Mayan king with the Mayan god of death on his hand. It's culturally relevant.

JANICE SU
College Student

Tell me about your doll.
It's an Asian ball-jointed doll made by a company called Cerberus Project. They're called Dollfies, which is like "doll" and "figure" combined, and they're very expensive, because they're made from polyurethane resin. His birthday is actually this month; he'll be a year old.

How expensive?
He cost $550 plus his wig was $30. It took me three years to save up, but he's totally worth every penny. He's just so special and lifelike. I'm currently saving up for another doll, and a friend's doll is staying with me while my friend is away at college.

Do you often dress alike?
The thing is, their outfits cost more than clothing for humans. I can't afford to buy my doll a forty-dollar T-shirt and fifty-dollar pants, so I'm just like, okay, I'll make clothing. And I made us these dinosaur hoodies. And then I made him jeans, and ripped the holes in them with scissors and pins and whatever.

Do you bring him everywhere?
I bring him to the movies, and sometimes when I go out to eat with my friends, I bring him, too. And I bring him to the park, but I don't bring him to school because it's too dangerous.

Does he get a lot of attention?
I get a lot of stares. Little kids say, "Mommy, I want one," and some people ask me why I carry a doll when I'm eighteen years old.

Why do you carry a doll?
He's an extension of me. I've met some of my best friends from carrying him around. We go to doll meets together; we hang out at Starbucks with our dolls. Those are the things that make me happy.

NICK LANDRUM
Audiobook Narrator, with Chatzie

What makes your voice good for reading aloud?
It's deep. People like that, especially if I go out drinking. And it's pleasant and sort of familiar. People tell me I sound like Andrew McCarthy. When I didn't have a beard, people told me I looked like him, too.

What's the last book you recorded?
Dearly Devoted Dexter. It's about a good serial killer who kills bad serial killers. It's really, really awful. I loathe it.

Have you done any that you like?
Bob Dylan's autobiography, the unabridged version. It doesn't get much press because Sean Penn did the abridged. But it was the fulfillment of a dream.

How would you describe your look?
Well, these are the Elvis glasses, which I always wear. His motto was "Taking care of business," so this is like "Taking care of business casual."

Where did you get this outfit?
The hat I got after I finished the Bob book as a gift to myself at J&J Hat Center. I'm follicly challenged, as Mr. Zellweger would say. Have you ever seen Kenny Chesney without a hat?

How about the dog?
The dog is an accessory as well as a sidekick. I was a little worried about being a straight guy with a small dog and an office in Chelsea, but things have been all right so far. A lot of models stop to talk to me.

And the rest?
I got the jacket at a vintage place called Metropolis. They specialize in rock-and-roll clothing and fruit boots.

What are fruit boots?
I'm from the South, where boots with zippers are frowned upon.

Does your wife help you shop?
She likes to dress me, which I'm fine with. She has very good taste. I like to say that I'm sleeping with my stylist rather than that I'm just whipped.

ANGEL GARCIA
High School Student

ANDRÉ J.
Muse

Aren't you cold?
No! Not at all. It's a mental thing. I woke up this morning feeling really spiritual, calm, easy, and free. I'm feeling lovely.

Is this an everyday outfit?
Oh, yes, it is! The blouse is Anna Sui, the shorts are vintage, and I'm wearing vintage sunglasses by Lanvin. And just, like, calmness. I'm wearing calmness. I'm very happy.

How did you get so happy?
Hard work. No longer living by anyone else's demands. I'm grown, I'm evolved, I can accept all that comes with being an individual.

What comes with being an individual?
In my case, trust, faith, hope, optimism, courage, wisdom, enthusiasm, and pizzazz.

Where did you come from?
Jersey. And I lived in L.A. up until a few years ago, when I just said, "Hmmm. Let's move to New York for the liberation, the freedom, the action. The life, the fashion, the glam." But I should point out that there is always a message behind the glam, and that message is, Become your dream.

What do you do?
I lip-synch, but I'm more of an example, an icon in my own right, a muse. I want people to look at me and feel inspired, to feel hope, to smile. I want to surge positive energy in your body, confirm that you too can be yourself.

Does it happen that way?
Oh, sure. I get some "Wow, oh my goodness, what the hell, you look fantastic, holla brotha" when I'm walking down the street, but my favorite thing I ever got was, "I am just so glad you're alive." I've had so many people say that to me, and that's what assists me on continuing my journey. I was put on this earth to be a bodhisattva, to just glow, emanate love, respect, peace, pizzazz. It's powerful.

DAVID RAUCH
Hedge-Fund Manager

What do you do?

I'm a money manager. I've been in the business thirteen years, and last year I started a small hedge fund.

Is there pressure to dress a certain way in finance?

I used to work at Bear Stearns, and you realize that you're making a lot of money and spending tons of it on clothes. Guys would come over and snip your tie in half if it was ugly. There wasn't anything written, but you definitely had a feeling of, Holy shit, I better get some nice shoes. It was like the Marines—a pretty badass place. I loved it.

Any room for individuality?

We used to go and get Ferragamo shoes with two buckles. The old guys would be like, "What are you doing? Are those Capezios?" Ace Greenberg, the executive committee chairman of Bear Stearns, is in a bow tie, but in our division, it was more "Don't get cute. No paisley."

Did you bring that mood to your new office?

I went to Europe for the first time last year—my wife's Swedish—and over there, you are in a suit and tie if you want to make money. In Manhattan, a billionaire could be in cutoffs. In Europe, you can tell who the rich people are. It's not like I'm superrich, but it's a mentality. If you're going to work, you should dress that way.

Where do you get your suits?

I'm six nine, so things have to be custom-made. My ex-girlfriend worked at Polo, so she would tell them we were engaged and I'd get Purple Label suits—that's what this one is. I still owe her for that. For shirts, I go to Phil's 1908 near Bloomingdale's. And at Bear Stearns, they used to send pretty girls from Tom James around and they would measure you in the conference room. One of them became a good friend, and I still get shirts from her.

Do you always wear a jacket and tie?

Yeah, for now anyway. But I went to Hiro the other night and I got grief at the door. The girl said, "Maybe you should take off the tie." I was expecting *Eyes Wide Shut,* but I got in and there were five guys in the corner wearing madras shirts.

Where do you get your suits?
I'm six nine, so things have to be custom-made.

177

CAROLINE PRINCE
Hairstylist

Why a star?

I hate that tattoo!
I got it five years ago
and it's way bigger than
I wanted. I was, like,
twenty years old and the
tattoo artist was eight
times bigger than me.
I didn't want to be a
pain in the ass.

ISABELLE LENFANT
Fashion Editor

KATE CHAPMAN
Gallery Assistant

SUNHWA CHUNG
Choreographer and Director

What are you doing today?
I'm going to Kmart to buy some milk for my baby. I live on Ninth Street between A and First Avenue, so it's very convenient.

What do you do?
I have a dance company, Ko-Ryo Dance Theater. The style is contemporary, but it's influenced by traditional Korean culture. I'm the choreographer, the director, and also I'm a full-time mom.

Tell me about your outfit.
I got the dress last year at a Korean H&M kind of store. I felt a little bit chilly in the morning when I put it on, so I put on a vintage petticoat underneath. Then, when I took my baby to school, all of the other parents were looking at me very strangely. I guess I look a little unusual.

Do you often dress unusually?
I like to stand out. My husband says that my eye for color is very vivid. I've noticed that most women wear jeans and black tops—the other day I went to a birthday party and every woman there was in that combination except for me.

Does being a dancer affect your fashion choices?
Yes, definitely. We're struggling all the time, but in a good way. There is a passion in transforming your body, and when you wear clothes, you need the freedom to express the passion.

How do you create a new dance?
Everything is inspired by my daily life. Maybe later I will make a dance about how I met you guys on the street today. That could be quite inspiring. The photographer was asking me to do very elegant movements, and I was really depressed before the picture, but afterward I thought, This was dance therapy!

HARRY BERNSTEIN
Advertising Art Director

What's this look?
I've been going for a cross between preppy and old-fashioned. The fedora is the old-fashioned part. What I like is when something is a little off, but not so off that I'm a circus freak. For me, originality is about taking two things that already exist and combining them. Like, hydrogen and oxygen making water.

Where did you get this outfit?
My hat I got vintage out in Williamsburg. My peacoat is Comme des Garçons. I bought it at If on Grand, and my glasses I got on Orchard Street. My scarf is from Century 21.

What do you do?
I've done ads for IBM, Kodak, Heineken. My most recent client, Boost, does urban stuff.

What's your favorite ad?
Nothing has inspired me lately—and I'm a very positive person! I feel like everything's being recycled.

What's the last thing that moved you?
Two summers ago, I drove cross-country, and I was in the White Sands desert of New Mexico. That left an impression on me. And I like photography—Gregory Crewdson, Katy Grannan. And I do listen to hip-hop, believe it or not. I like the whole Houston scene.

How did you get into that?
When you grow up in New York you think you're in the cultural epicenter, but, like, the South! It's this whole thing! I've been dating girls from the South, and I worry about being Harry Bernstein.

Describe your look.
I look like a combo of Woody Allen and Howard Stern, see? But I'm not Jewish, I'm Catholic. No one believes me. And I'm like, "My mom's Catholic; those are the rules!" By Jewish law, I'm not Jewish, but I could definitely roll in South Williamsburg. And they love me in B&H.

Describe your look.
I look like a combo of Woody Allen and Howard Stern, see? But I'm not Jewish, I'm Catholic. No one believes me.

**SOPHIA RUBIO AND
ESTRELLA MARTINEZ**
Actress and Dental Hygienist

What's going on with the dinosaur hats?

We went to the American Museum of Natural History yesterday, and then we went out all day and all night. We spent the night at a friend's house and we just got up. We haven't even showered or brushed our teeth or anything, so we just thought, let's wear the hats.

BOBBY VITA
Electrical Contractor

What do you do, Bobby?
I'm from Queens. Astoria. I own my own electrical company.

What are you wearing today?
My sunglasses are Prada. The tracksuit's Armani.

It says Puma.
It's Armani.

And how about that jewelry?
You mean my Rolex? I like class and style. I like to look good.

Where did you get it all?
Down in the district. The diamond district.

Have you always bought yourself jewelry?
Yeah. My whole life.

Is there anyone whose style you admire?
Versace. Al Pacino. Bobby De Niro.

Where'd you get that tan?
In Florida. Hollywood. I went twice already this month. I have a condo down there. I like to go lay in the sun, go out for fish.

Do you ever wear sunblock?
Absolutely not.

What product do you use in your hair?
I'm growing my hair, honey. I use gel.

What's the last movie you saw?
A porno. *Caught from Behind.*

What do you do in your spare time?
You want to know what I do in my spare time, honey? I express my feelings with all sorts of women. I go to Yankees games. I hang out. I go have dinner. I go have lunch. Union dinners, union lunches.

What do you think of that inflatable rat the unions use?
I think it's terrible. They're legitimate gangsters.

Does that make it hard to get work done?
Not for me, but it could definitely get complicated for others.

Why not for you?
You've seen the pictures.

What product do you use in your hair?
I'm growing my hair, honey. I use gel.

IAN BRADLEY
D.J.

ARMANDO COLONDRES
Bachelor

LISA JO
Artist

How would you describe your style?
It's difficult. I try to keep it a little mix of vintage and new, and high-waisted everything is all I wear. I don't think I'm too flashy. I like to be classic and elegant. I don't know if these diaper shorts are very elegant, but still.

What are you doing today?
Apartment hunting. I'm having a wretched time of it. Brooklyn's a little tough, and brokers definitely take advantage of a young girl trying to live alone. They're awful.

What's the worst thing a broker's done to you?
Point out small details, like electrical outlets and the number of bulbs around the bathroom mirror. Brokers just assume that a girl looking for an apartment by herself is worried about vanity mirrors and where to plug in her hair dryer.

Where do you want to live?
Greenpoint. I'm an artist, so I need studio space. Williamsburg is a little too crowded and loud for me, but I want to be near the L train.

Do you dress a certain way to apartment hunt?
Not really, but I think you should look more serious so people can take you seriously.

Are you fussy about grooming?
I keep it simple. I love L'Occitane products, a little Chanel eyeliner, and that's it.

What kind of art do you do?
A little bit of everything. Right now I'm making watercolors of really tiny little buffaloes. I do some video work as well. I'm from California, a place called Palos Verdes, which is a small suburb near L.A. I think I miss the West, but not necessarily Los Angeles, which is why my work is leaning toward the Wild West.

Who's your favorite artist?
Right now, Rodney Graham. I am drawn to artists with a sense of humor. Rodney Graham deals with lapse of time and perspective in a really comical way.

What do you miss most about the West?
Well, I have this weird nostalgia for the Old West. But at this point in my life, what I really miss is Mexican food. No one can make a decent enchilada here.

JOHN HOWARD KNIGHT III, AKA "TRÉ"
Designer

How do you get your hair like that?
My friend Paul does it once a week. He puts gel on my hair while it's dry, and then he combs it through. Then he shapes it with a comb and his fingers, and then I bake under the dryer for 45 minutes. It gets really, really solid, like a helmet.

How did you get the idea for it?
I got the idea from the twenties and the thirties. I used to have a white, white mohawk, but it was just so damaging to my hair, so I cut it all off and went to Paul and was all, "What can I do with my hair?" I love it because when I wake up in the morning, my hair's already done.

What inspires the rest of your style?
Well, this is just my day look. When I go out, I have a whole different category of looks, and I'm usually corseted. A casual night outfit would be tights, a pair of heels, and then maybe a collared shirt with a corset over that. Some people would consider my style to be gothic, but those are people who just don't really get it.

So what is it, then?
It's period driven, but with a modern touch. It stems from the past and is inspired by art and other things. It's my own vision. The thing is, I'm kind of like a chameleon. I think that's my favorite feature of my style.

Where are you from?
I'm a Southern boy at heart. I'm from Chapel Hill, North Carolina.

Do you bring this look down South?
The corsets are just for night and for New York, but I don't feel like you should ever change who you are when you change your environment. It's just helping other people be more accepting. Even if I walk down the street and get a lot of "what the fuck is that?"—I just smile, I keep on walking and keep on doing it, because no one's ever going to get it if I don't.

HELEN MIRREN
Actor

BEN NARDOLILLI
Student

That's quite a mustache.

I started growing facial hair when I was 10, which is really a blessing and a curse. It grows so fast that it gets out of control very quickly. But I can't really be clean-shaven, either, because I'd have to shave again by lunchtime.

Do you always wear a mustache?

I had grown an Abraham Lincoln beard this winter—no mustache—but it just didn't feel right. And it started getting warmer, so I switched.

Do people treat you differently depending on your facial hair?

Definitely. When I have a full beard, I get treated like I'm much older. I study history and philosophy at NYU. If I wear a suit, people assume that I'm a teacher, which I love. I'll go into a classroom, and everyone will just be waiting for me to start talking.

Do you have style icons?

For a while, John Travolta in *Saturday Night Fever* was really big for me. But now I'm just sort of into male fashions of the seventies. It was bold. It wasn't all about a blue shirt and a pair of khaki pants.

Where did you get the hat and sunglasses?

I have absolutely no idea where the sunglasses came from. The hat I took from my high school drama department. Together, they just became my thing. People say, "Why are you wearing that?" And I say, "It's my look."

What are you doing this summer?

I teach at a camp for the academically gifted at UVA. Last summer, I tried to teach them comparative government, and they all wrote their own constitutions. One group declared themselves Marxist. Another group created a reverse Taliban where men couldn't do anything. This summer, I think we're going to get into free will. That might be dangerous for 12-year-olds.

Do you have style icons?

For a while, John Travolta in *Saturday Night Fever* was really big for me.

LACHLAN MCLEOD
Removalist

What do you do?
The last thing I did was a Budweiser
advertisement. I had to pretend I was in
a band that had just finished playing and
had gone out to drink a beer. We had to
drink Budweiser.

Do you like Budweiser?
No.

Are you an actor?
No. They just needed someone very
quickly and somebody saw me walking
down the street. I guess they were looking
for a particular look.

What look is that?
I'm not entirely sure. I'm a bit gaunt, you
know, and people seem to think there's
something dramatic about that.

And your style?
Well, I'm a pretty eclectic dresser. All of my
clothes come from thrift stores and always
have. I'm forty-three now, and I've been
dressing this way since I was sixteen. Have
you ever looked at a crowd from fifty or
sixty years ago and noticed that there isn't
anybody without a hat on? I don't even
like hats, but it seems as if in those days
people dressed up. Clothing nowadays
reminds me of adult baby wear: baggy,
functional, dull.

**So Budweiser stopped you and we
stopped you. Do you get stopped
a lot?**
I do. It's usually Japanese tourists, though.
They think I'm Vincent Gallo.

If you're not an actor, what do you do?
I like the idea of researching more than
anything. I'm just very interested in
history. I've been studying history for a
long time. I know it sounds really vague,
but it's something like that.

So you research history all day?
And I'm a removalist. If you're moving,
you put things in boxes and I'll come and
move them into vans. Keeps me in shape.

KAMALIE GORDON
Rap Musician

DEENA ABDULAZIZ
Mother

Where do you live?
For a long time, we were only here, on the Upper West Side, but now we are also back in Riyadh. It's important for my husband. I'm sure you understand.

Do you like living between the two cities?
I love every single thing about New York. I even love having a hot dog! But I love the desert in Riyadh—it's home, it's family, and it's stable.

What do you do?
I have three kids: a five-year-old girl and twin boys, who are three.

Where did you get your . . .
The skirt is Proenza Schouler, the T-shirt is Prada. The shoes are Miu Miu, and the bag is Hermès, of course. The charms are Prada. I'm a little bit of a Prada whore. The necklace is Lanvin, and the watch is Cartier.

That's a lot of fashion. Are you particular about your beauty regime, too?
Well, yes. The shampoo is Kerastase, the moisturizer is Peter Thomas Roth. I start with his glycolic moisturizer, and then I do a lot of blendings, mostly with Armani bronzer fluid. For lipstick, I use glosses. I'm very ashamed to say this, but I really like the Jessica Simpson ones because they taste so good.

And perfume?
I blend an incense from my country that is very expensive per ounce. It's the essential oil used in the most expensive perfumes. It's not even amber—it's a lot stronger than that. It's a type of tree. I blend it with Fleur de Cassis by Frédéric Malle that I buy at Barneys, and also his Musc Ravageur body oil.

You really love fashion. Do you like fashiony movies?
Of course! *Breakfast at Tiffany's, Auntie Mame, All About Eve, Eyes of Laura Mars* are my all-time favorites.

Did you see *Fahrenheit 9/11*?
I think it was very biased, but pro-democracy. It's anti-Bush, which is okay; even his criticism of the Saudis I can understand. I might not agree with it, but I understand it.

So who do you want to win?
As a Saudi, Bush, but as an American, Kerry.

Are you particular about your beauty regime?
Well, yes. I'm very ashamed to say this, but I really like the Jessica Simpson glosses because they taste so good.

NEVILLE WAKEFIELD
Writer

PETER MCGOUGH
Artist

You smell so strongly of lavender.
My wonderful friend has a salon on East 3rd Street called Grace Heavens. She is a naturalist. I smell so good because of her, and also, lavender helps you with your mood.

Do you always look so antique?
My look has changed over the years. In the eighties, we were very particular about antique clothes, but now they're harder to find and they fall apart. But we were very strict: the summer was white linen, fall was tweed, and in winter we were in black. When you're twenty-two and you weigh 120 pounds, you can wear a lot of vintage.

How did you get into that?
I used to wear my father's old suits from the forties when I was growing up upstate. It was the seventies, and there I was in forties suits. And then I met my partner McDermott and he had this whole group of people who only dressed as if they lived in the past. So elegant! And slimming! It makes people look so much better. I mean, come on, can you imagine Cary Grant in a tracksuit? Cary Grant is my idol of clothes.

Any other idols?
Well, in *I Love Lucy*, Lucy has to go to the doctor one night and she says, "I've never worn jeans on the subway and I'm not about to." The way people dress now is just hideous.

Do you ever buy new clothes?
I've had all my clothes for at least twenty-five years. Do I need to buy another article of clothing because suddenly fashion is up, down, left, right? Absolutely not. It's a sucker's game, fashion. People are suckers. I mean, skinny jeans? I guess it keeps people entertained so they don't have to think about war. The only thing I buy new is underwear: Brooks Brothers boxer shorts with a button waist.

Is there a uniform there?

There's a dress code, but I never follow it. We have to wear collared shirts. I don't own any collared shirts. And my skirts and pants are always, like, sequins or leopard prints. No one else dresses like me at school.

How does everyone else dress?

On the preppier side. Poly Prep is known for its athletics, and there's a lot of kids from Staten Island, so they shop at the mall.

Do you hang with the preppy kids?

Most of my friends with the same interests go to other schools. When you go to a concert, you're going to meet people like you, whereas at school, everyone's stranded.

Tell me about this outfit.

I got my eyeglasses at a store on East Ninth Street called Fabulous Fanny's. The cowboy boots were my mom's. I just started wearing them about a year ago. The tights are from Anna Sui. The skirt I bought I don't know where, but I cut out pieces of fabric and had them sewn on at the dry cleaner. The T-shirt I got on eBay. I resewed it to make it fit properly.

Are you very into Jimi Hendrix?

In the seventh grade I randomly bought a CD, and that was the start of it. He was really psychedelic.

Do you have any style icons?

Right now I like Marc Bolan from T. Rex. I switch every week, though. I also like Frida Kahlo a lot. I dressed up as her for Halloween.

What are you reading?

I love *Tristessa,* by Jack Kerouac, and *Nausea,* by Jean-Paul Sartre—but I can't pronounce it. And I like James Baldwin.

Movies?

One of my favorites has to be *Rocky,* which is unexplainable because I don't like sports and I don't like muscular people. But it makes me really happy.

What's on your lunchbox?

It's the Beatles—*Yellow Submarine.* My mom bought it for me for Christmas. People always say it should be kept in the closet because it's a relic of the past, but it wasn't that expensive. I use it as a purse.

Do you ever wish you lived in a different decade?

I would have loved to live in the sixties or late seventies. It's kind of pathetic, and I feel bad about that, but what are you going to do?

JARVIS WONG
Architect

Why do all architects have those glasses?
It started with Corbusier. Mine are from Oliver Peoples. I like them because they define my face, which is fairly nondescript. In a sense, my glasses "crossimilate" with my more general design principles regarding how to play materials against color and proportion.

How do you describe your style?
I call myself an "Urban Nerd."

What does that mean?
It's kind of subtle. I mix different ideas that I come across, and then turn them into my personal stuff.

Does the way you dress correspond to your work?
It definitely relates. My style is minimal eclectic, in the sense that the architecture itself is minimal, and then the accessories come from different styles and periods.

Tell me about this outfit.
The shirt is custom-made by an old tailor in Hong Kong: Swiss cotton, French cut. The trousers, which I guess you'd call pencil pants, were custom-made as well. The shoes are suede sneakers from Sperry Top-Sider. They have them exclusively at Jeffrey. The belt and the watch are Hermès, and they're my basics. I wear my underwear, I wear my Hermès watch. Every day.

What are you listening to on your iPod?
Goldfrapp. She's like the 21st-century Debbie Harry. I like to listen to her and Coldplay together. It's like everything: Whatever works!

How do you describe your style?
I call myself an "Urban Nerd."

LISA FALCONE
Writer, with Liliana and Carolina

How old are your daughters?
They're 9 months old, and they're twins.
I did IVF and got pregnant with them on
the third try. Isn't technology wonderful?

Do you have other children as well?
I have three other kids—my pooches,
Venus, Aphrodite, and Zena. Two Yorkies
and a Chihuahua. We're five girls and
a boy.

What are you doing today?
We were just visiting Dad. Sometimes,
when my husband works late, I'll bring
the girls over the next day. We do a feeding
there in his office. He runs a hedge fund—
but believe me, when we met, we had
no cash!

What do you do?
I started out modeling. When I met my
husband, I started freelance editing, and
now I'm writing a novel.

What's it about?
I can't tell you. It's inspired by a true story,
it will be published anonymously, and I
will donate all the money to kids.

How do you describe your style?
Life is colorful! This is a Valentino jacket,
a Prada sweater, and Prada boots. I collect
things, I shop at the flea market, and I'm
really good at trunk shows. And I work
around things well. For example, I'm a
vegetarian, but I'll wear leather because
it could be killed for meat. Therefore, I'm
being an environmentalist. And I love fur,
but I buy mine at the flea market and only
if it's 50 years old, because 50 years ago
we were not familiar with the way they kill
animals. And I borrowed Liliana's dress
from Oscar de la Renta recently.

What do you mean?
I bought a dress at Oscar de la Renta that
reminds me of Liliana. It's like a cupcake.
I put it in a box with a note telling her
all about the night I wore it. When the
girls turn 18, I will give them the keys to
a storage space. I'm putting all sorts of
things in it.

**Do you always dress your daughters so
beautifully?**
Yes. Today they're wearing Bonpoint
dresses, shoes from Flora and Henri,
and blouses from Barneys. When they're
sleeping, I plan their outfits for the next
day. I constantly see kids dressed casual,
and I just feel that if I teach my kids to be
casual, then fashion will die. And I'm not
going to let that happen on my watch!

**Do you always dress your
daughters so beautifully?**
Yes. I just feel
that if I teach my
kids to be casual,
then fashion
will die.

THELMA SCHNITZER
Opera Lover

What are you up to today?
There was a terrible draft at the opera last night, so I'm not feeling too sharp, but I wanted to walk up Madison Avenue, and to make it at least as far as Valentino.

Where do you live?
In New York, the St. Regis. We always come for the opera, and we get the Astor Suite. They remember things: We like the blankets instead of the duvets, that sort of thing. We have three homes, and I think three is enough.

How would you describe your look?
I guess you would call it fussy. I was brought up in that era of suits and dresses with coats, and that is the way I continue to dress. I have a drawer, and I bet I have 50 pairs of gloves in it. All kinds, from the wrist to above the elbow.

What's changed most about the city in all these years?
People don't dress! It's not just New York. You used to go to Paris and get dressed. Now it's blue jeans and a Chanel jacket.

Where'd you get your suit?
Chanel—it's from last season. It looks off-white, but it's actually beige.

What's your favorite opera?
An old warhorse: *La Traviata*.

Do you ever listen to anything other than opera?
Chopin is my great love.

How about rap music?
Rap music! Even my grandchildren are old, you know.

Where'd you get those sunglasses?
I don't know, but they say Jackie O. inside.

And the lipstick?
I like a red lipstick, specifically Chanel Rose Stone, which they just stopped making. I only have one left.

Who does your hair?
In New York, I always go to the Pierre Hotel. My hairdresser is Toni—a lady named Toni! It looks like a simple hairdo, but it isn't that easy.

How on earth have you stayed married for 66 years?
It's just being polite to each other always.

What's changed most about the city in all these years?
People don't dress! It's not just New York. You used to go to Paris and get dressed. Now it's blue jeans and a Chanel jacket.

JEZIAH ROBERTSON, 7, AND DAKOTAROME PAUL, 6,
Cousins

Do you guys always wear suits?

JEZIAH (LEFT): No. But I like it. You get to be handsome, and you get to be calm and stuff. And people get to compliment you and tell you all sorts of things about your suit. Like, how they like your shoes.

DAKOTA: For school, I wear a uniform. Sometimes people think I'm, like, 40, but I'm 6. But I love wearing a suit 'cause I look sharp! Like I'm a model. And people are like, "Dakota! You look so nice! I want to be like you someday!"

What grade are you in?

JEZIAH: I'm in third grade, and that's good so far.

DAKOTA: First grade. I'm learning how to read big books, like the Bible.

Do you play sports?

JEZIAH: I like to play football. The Giants are my favorite, and the Deadskins.

The Redskins?

I used to think it was called that, but it's called the Deadskins.

How about movies?

I like hero movies, you know, movies that have a hero in them. And Disney. Just stuff that's not age-inappropriate.

Do you like to shop?

DAKOTA: It's so fun. I get to pick out my hats. Like, Yankees hats in all different colors. And my pants, like my Sean John jeans and stuff. And my sneakers. I like Jordans, and Uptowns. They're Nikes.

Is there anyone you'd like to dress like when you're an adult?

JEZIAH: I'd like to be fixed up like my dad always does it. With braids and stuff. I want to be calm like him. And I try to act like one of those guys on TV that has nice suits and stuff when you go out. Like I won an award or something.

THE
LISTINGS

NOLITA

Nolita can seem like one of
the city's most intimidating
shopping neighborhoods:
It's all terribly hip, and
everyone on the street
looks fantastic.

WHERE TO SHOP

1 **Steven Alan**
229 Elizabeth St, bet. Prince
and Houston Sts.
212-226-7482
stevenalan.com

2 **Seize sur Vingt**
243 Elizabeth St. bet. Prince
and Houston Sts.
212-343-0476
16sur20.com

3 **Zero Maria Cornejo**
225 Mott St. nr. Spring St.
212-925-3849
zeromariacornejo.com

4 **A Détacher**
262 Mott St. nr. Houston St.
212-625-3380

5 **Calypso**
252 Mott St. bet. Prince and
Houston Sts.
212-965-0990
calypso-celle.com

6 **Sigerson Morrison**
28 Prince St. at Mott St.
212-219-3893
sigersonmorrison.com

7 **Lyell**
173 Elizabeth St. nr. Spring St.
212-966-8484

8 **Unis**
226 Elizabeth St. nr. Prince St.
212-431-5533

9 **Henry Lehr**
9 Prince St. at Elizabeth St.
212-274-9921

10 **Malia Mills**
199 Mulberry St. nr. Spring St.
212-625-2311
maliamills.com

11 **Resurrection**
217 Mott St. bet. Prince and
Spring Sts.
212-625-1374
resurrectionvintage.com

Kate Young (see pages 64–65), spotted
on the corner of Prince and Mott Streets.

The corner of Prince and Mott is one of
our all-time favorite Look Book locations;
it's where we met Kosuke, for example,
and also Brian Ermanski. Nolita is also
what people want from shopping in
New York, with small, designer-run
boutiques and nice little places to have
lunch. It's not bling-y down there (which
is not to say that it's cheap—it's not); but
it's got an insider feel. The thing to do
in Nolita is to be inspired by what you
see walking down the street as much as
you're inspired by what's in the shops.
And don't get depressed if the shop
assistants all look younger than you,
thinner than you, and far better dressed.
They are. Just think of it as inspiration.

Elizabeth Street is men's shirt mecca:
It's home to both **Steven Alan** and
Seize sur Vingt. One very stylish guy
I am lucky to know explains it to me
like this: "No one would ever wear
both. You have to decide which you are:
floppy or finished." I'm not so strict in
my tastes—you can switch it up every
once in a while!—but it's true that the
two stores represent diametrically
opposite aesthetics. Steven Alan shirts
are legendarily soft: twisted placards,
inverted seams. They're the shirts of

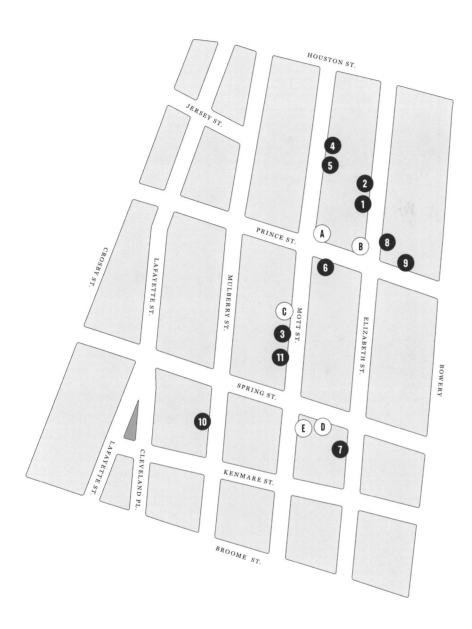

HOUSTON ST.

JERSEY ST.

PRINCE ST.

CROSBY ST.

LAFAYETTE ST.

MULBERRY ST.

MOTT ST.

ELIZABETH ST.

BOWERY

SPRING ST.

LAFAYETTE ST.

CLEVELAND PL.

KENMARE ST.

BROOME ST.

WHERE TO EAT

(A)

Café Gitane always seems on the verge of jumping the shark: too many people dressed up for mere cous cous and a cup of tea. But just when you think you can't bear another pair of aviators or aspirational bedhead, the place redeems itself because it's good and cheap and friendly, which is all you want from a neighborhood café anyway. *242 Mott Street at Prince St. (212-334-9552)*

(B)

Skip the line on Elizabeth Street, which could take over your entire afternoon, and get a chicken mole sandwich, an ear of corn, and lemonade from **Café Habana**'s take-out counter next door. The best looking boys in the neighborhood always do. *17 Prince Street at Elizabeth St. (212-625-2002)*

(C) (D)

How can one not love restaurants named after carbs? First, there was **Rice**: with a zillion kinds of rice (red, black, green, and so on) and delicious bits to eat it with, like chicken satay or lentil soup; and then came **Bread** right around the corner: Italian food served light, with amazing salads. *Rice: 227 Mott Street, between Spring and Prince Sts. (212-226-5775); Bread: 20 Spring Street, between Mott and Elizabeth Sts. (212-334-1015)*

(E)

The Italian couple that owns **Epistrophy** is so good looking that the laid-back bar-and-snacks spot could easily owe its success to their Roman noses and excellent tans. But it's actually terrifically comfortable and pleasant for a glass of wine. *200 Mott Street, between Kenmare and Spring Sts. (212-966-0904)*

choice for filmmakers, say, and rumpled novelists. They look best when tossed in the machine and allowed to air dry. Seize sur Vingt's shirts are far more finished: worn, perhaps, by the grooviest banker on the floor. Or on your wedding day.

Every year during Fashion Week, I see the coolest of the French editors slipping into **Zero Maria Cornejo** between shows. The clothes here sometimes look scary on the hangers—Belgian, even—but on, they are heaven. They're sleek and modern but also cozy. The palette is usually neutral, though each season there's a shot of something bright.

There are perfect sweater dresses and jersey tunics with bubble hems, brilliant for layering. I sometimes feel that the great genius and secret of Zero is that you get to be as comfy as any soccer mom in her drawstring velour pants, but still look hip while you're at it.

A Détacher is Nolita at its best. It's run by the designer, Mona Kowalska. Her workroom is in the back of her shop, and she rarely sells her clothes elsewhere. They are so glamorous, so sophisticated, so grown up; I always imagine that if I were the director of some great, avant garde museum, I would shop here only.

Kozuke (see pages 104–105), photographed on the corner of Prince and Mott Sts.

_____

Also: A Détacher is full of wonderful little finds—a sea urchin-like dish scrubber, for example, or an antique diamond ring—that make you want to re-do your whole house around a tea cup.

Although it's become a national phenomenon in the past few years, Mott Street is **Calypso's** original New York home, and the shop smells always of gardenias. Somehow, it's always vacation-time in Calypso: the salesgirls are showing off their impossibly flat and tan bellies, gussied up in fruit-salad colors like nectarine and plum. I've always liked Calypso because it's so easy, but I really fell in love with it while profiling the owner, Christiane Celle, for the magazine last year. A friend of mine who was struggling with her weight welled up with tears when I mentioned what I was writing about: Calypso fits just about everyone, and they'll never make you feel bad about your body.

Sigerson Morrison is the Nolita shoe pioneer. A lot of people complain about the quality of the shoes, but I've never had a problem. They're incredible with color.

There's not a tremendous selection at **Lyell**, which means it can be hit or miss, but it's a lovely spot to linger regardless. It's so extremely feminine, almost twenties in effect, overflowing with sexy secretary blouses, pencil skirts, and vintage shoes. There's this one amazing dress—the deer dress—that's become a perennial, and which cries out, like so much of Lyell's clothing does, for red lipstick and those stockings with a seam up the back.

The selection at **Unis** varies, but their army jacket is a neighborhood classic. I can't promise you'll find much more than that, but if you're looking for an Army jacket, perhaps that's enough.

No one particularly likes shopping for jeans, but at **Henry Lehr** it's as painless as it can be. There's a really good selection, and the salespeople are nice about sorting through the piles for you.

What's wonderful about **Malia Mills**, which is a bathing-suit shop, is that no one there will make you feel fat, flat, or too dimpled for the beach. The brand's ad campaigns have starred "real" women (a term I loathe, as models are, in fact, "real" as well, but you know what I mean) since Dove was known as an old-lady bar of soap. The sizing is done by bra size, and there's something to accommodate everyone from As to double Ds.

Resurrection sells fancy, designer vintage clothing from a number of eras. It's not cheap—you're more likely to find a seventies Halston that's red carpet ready than you are to find a label-less sundress for nice and cheap.

SOHO

Soho is a shopping zoo. It's best to avoid it on the weekends, when the crowds are large and unyielding, but during the week it's quiet and lovely to wander up and down the cobblestone streets.

Andre J from the "Fli High Fli Guys" (see pages 54–57), spotted on Prince St. and Broadway.

The area is loaded with the same luxury chains you'll find uptown, along Madison Avenue, and it's a great mystery to most New Yorkers how anyone still thinks of the neighborhood as "funky."

That said, there's fantastic style to be found in Soho, always. We've had very successful shoots on the busy corner of Broadway and Prince. It's where we met André J., wearing his hot pants on a February afternoon, and Helen Mirren on her way to lunch. The Fli High Fli Guys cruise Soho in the afternoons, showing off their clever combinations.

A.P.C. is a sort of uniform for both genders in certain circles: The clothes are neither expensive nor complicated but remain somehow hip. It's Gap for the groovy. Jeans at A.P.C. are a specific and culty thing: They are stiff and unadorned and come with a special list of care instructions that range from "never wash" to "roll about in the sand." People—guys, in particular—are maniacal about their A.P.C. jeans, and consider a well-worn pair a serious badge of cool.

Kirna Zabête is a multi-label fashion shop for people who really, truly love clothes. The upstairs is full of the designers you read about in the front pages of *Vogue*—Sari Gueron, Peter Som—as well as heavy-hitters like Chloe, Lanvin, and Ungaro. Downstairs, it's a little less expensive, and also there are treats like candy and fantastic dog leashes. The owners of Kirna Zabête are a bubbly pair of Southern sorority sisters (Kirna and Zebête are their nicknames) who take the whole hospitality thing very seriously, which makes it a pleasant place to shop. They also have great sales in the periods between seasons: Look downstairs in the back.

There are several branches of **Wolford** in the city, but the Soho one always seems well-stocked. Wolford stockings are, simply put, the best, and they cross all sorts of fashion lines: Glamorous uptown dowagers wear them, as do their glamorous downtown counterparts. If it makes you ill to spend so much on a single pair of tights, know that they do tend to last through the season. Polar tights are a fashion editor's secret during the winter shows: stock up early.

"Haute Hippie" isn't everyone's look, but if it's yours, there's no better place to shop than **Dosa**. There are slip dresses, drawstring pants, and soft cashmere sweaters in gentle,

WHERE TO SHOP

1 A.P.C.
131 Mercer St. bet. Prince and Spring Sts.
212-966-9685
apc.fr

2 Kirna Zabête
96 Greene St. nr. Spring St.
212-941-9656
kirnazabete.com

3 Wolford
122 Greene St. at Prince St.
212-343-0808
wolford.com

4 Dosa
107 Thompson St. nr. Prince St.
212-431-1733
dosainc.com

5 Legacy
109 Thompson St. nr. Prince St.
212-966-4827
legacy-nyc.com

6 Makie
109 Thompson St. nr. Prince St.
212-625-3930
makieclothier.com

7 A Bathing Ape
91 Greene St. nr. Spring St.
212-925-0222
bape.com

8 Jill Stuart
100 Greene St. nr. Spring St.
212-343-2300
jillstuart.com

9 IF Soho
94 Grand St. at Greene St.
212-334-4964

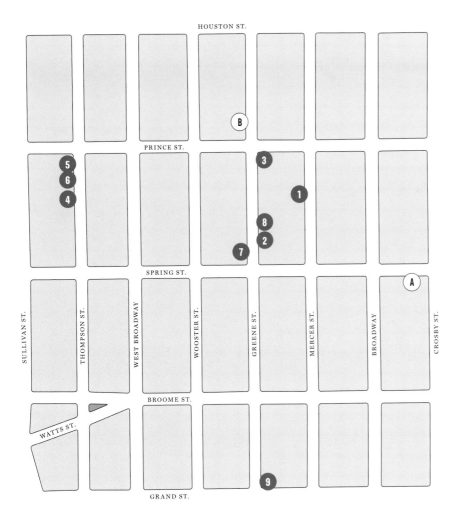

HOUSTON ST.

PRINCE ST.

SPRING ST.

BROOME ST.

WATTS ST.

GRAND ST.

SULLIVAN ST. · THOMPSON ST. · WEST BROADWAY · WOOSTER ST. · GREENE ST. · MERCER ST. · BROADWAY · CROSBY ST.

WHERE TO EAT

A

Great Soho shopping days are capped off with oysters at **Balthazar**, accompanied by a good eyeing of everyone else's shopping bags. It's particularly fantastic during the holidays, when there are Christmas lights strung up and everyone is (or seems to be) in a fantastic mood. *80 Spring St. nr. Crosby St. (212-965-1785 balthazarbakery.com)*

B

Kelley and Ping always strikes me as a perfect Soho place because it's lofty, unpretentious, and still, somehow, fabulous. It's a noodle shop, really, but a glamorous one. *127 Greene St. bet. Prince and Houston Sts. (212-228-1212 eatrice.com)*

shimmery colors. These are clothes for people who like yoga and soy milk: I would imagine that Republicans are gently turned away at the door.

Legacy, right beside Dosa, has never been flashy, but it's always been there. It's a shop that mixes vintage and new quite easily, and has a somewhat unusual collection of jewelry and shoes. There's never much in terms of choice at Legacy, but for people who like boutique shopping and have a nostalgic bent when it comes to fashion choices, it's ideal.

Whether or not teeny, tiny little children need elegant clothing is a matter of personal discretion. For those who do, **Makie** is perfect. It's a small shop run by a Japanese couple, and while the clothes are expensive, they are still childlike. They are what perfect, apple-cheeked children wear in storybooks, and also in the Baby Bjorns of well-dressed parents.

A Bathing Ape is a Japanese streetwear phenomenon that is starting to catch on here. Some larger grapevine of cool announces when the sweatshirt/sneaker/anorak of the moment arrives, and there's always a line down the block.

One of the best vintage stores in New York is not a vintage store at all, but rather, it's the basement of **Jill Stuart**. Stuart started collecting lacy, racy vintage dresses as inspiration, and then started selling them on their own, as is, mended and sorted and fixed. She tends to choose the more romantic: lace collars and high necks, for anyone with a thing for Edith Wharton or Scott Fitzgerald heroines.

IF Soho stocks the kind of clothes that brave women wear: women who aren't afraid to cut their hair short, sport bold glasses, and hunormous jewelry. There's a strong Japanese influence at IF: Comme des Garçons is always well represented, as are curious shapes. Clothes as *objets*.

LOWER EAST SIDE

When the word
"gentrification" is spoken
in New York, the Lower
East Side often springs
to mind.

Michael D'Andrade (see pages 30–31),
photographed at the corner of
Orchard and Rivington Sts.

Luxury condos are going up beside the low-income projects, and the neighborhood's old Eastern European and South American shops are being replaced by all sorts of multi-starred foodie magnets and groovy places to shop.

There are fantastic vintage stores that pay homage to the area's rock-and-roll history, which is why Monique Garofalo and her mom were looking for sixties concert tees. There are lots of new, too-cool sneaker shops as well. The best comment we ever heard about the Lower East Side came from Michael D'Andrade, who's spent his entire life living at the corner of Delancey and Grand. He told me, "If I were to go to Michigan, I'd have a good time and all that, but I wouldn't try to act like a native."

Sneaker fetish is well documented among lots of different style sets. There are the B-boys who clean their Air Force Ones daily with a soft toothbrush and a touch of bleach, and there are the indy rockers who like their Adidas vintage. They all find sneaker bliss at **Alife Rivington Club**. The great joy of Alife is discovering it for the first time. Set in a grungy and unremarkable tenement, the sneakers are treated like great works of art, displayed reverentially in a rich wood display case.

WHERE TO SHOP

1 Alife Rivington Club
158 Rivington St. nr. Clinton St.
212-375-8128
rivingtonclub.com

**2 Freemans
Sporting Club**
8 Rivington St. bet. Bowery and
Chrystie St.
212-673-3209

3 Foley & Corinna
114 Stanton St. bet. Essex and
Ludlow Sts.
212-529-2338
www.foleyandcorinna.com

4 TG-170
170 Ludlow St. bet. Stanton and
Houston Sts.
212-995-8660
tg170.com

5 Peggy Pardon
153 Ludlow St. bet. Rivington
and Stanton Sts.
212-529-3686
peggypardon.com

6 Jutta Neumann
158 Allan St. bet. Rivington and
Stanton Sts.
212-982-7048
juttaneumann-newyork.com

7 Orchard Corset
157 Orchard St. bet. Rivington
and Stanton Sts.
212-674-0786

HOUSTON ST.

ELDRIDGE ST.

ALLEN ST.

ORCHARD ST.

LUDLOW ST.

STANTON ST.

ESSEX ST.

NORFOLK ST.

SUFFOLK ST.

CLINTON ST.

ATTORNEY ST.

RIVINGTON ST.

ALLEN ST.

DELANCEY ST.

They do have a good, constantly updated collection, but truthfully, you could find a lot of this stuff elsewhere. But nowhere else will you feel quite as groovy doing it.

First there was a restaurant, then a mysterious boys' club in the basement, and now there's **Freemans Sporting Club**, the store with a subway-tiled "olde fashioned" barber shop in back. Yes, it's pretentious: all about guys who spend several hours every morning working on looking "rugged" and "masculine." It's as if by surrounding oneself with the traditional totems of manhood— taxidermy trophies and rusty old shaving kits—an interest in fashion becomes firmly heterosexual and butch. But analysis aside, the shirts are simple and good. Taken without their carefully styled surroundings, they'd just be shirts, but everyone needs shirts. Right?

Foley & Corinna sells half vintage clothing and half "vintage-inspired" clothing. Stick with the former, as its quality tends to be higher. It's not fancy vintage, like you find at Resurrection on Mott Street, but everyday vintage: little paisley dresses and hippie tops for wearing to rock shows at Pianos.

WHERE TO EAT

(A)

Clinton St. Baking Company is all about eggs, French toast, and tall, tall sandwiches. If it wasn't in such a trendy neighborhood, it would be your corner café, but it is, so there's often a wait to eat the (admittedly good versions of) pretty standard stuff. *4 Clinton St. at E. Houston St. (646-602-6263 clintonstreetbaking.com)*

(B)

Le Père Pinard is a French café with a lovely garden that seems authentically Parisian. The food is average, but it's happy-making inside, the kind of place that gives spiritual permission to drink at lunch. *175 Ludlow St. nr. Stanton St. (212-777-4917 leperepinard.com)*

TG-170 is a neighborhood institution. These are clothes for girls who wear messenger bags as opposed to handbags and believe deeply that a pair of Chuck Taylors matches all. The clothes are feminine, but not so much that you couldn't ride your bicycle between gigs in them.

Peggy Pardon is a tiny vintage shop that is well curated and, thankfully, never smells of mothballs. While the merchandise shifts constantly, the great emphasis is on dresses, and on dressing up. It's not so outrageous as to be costume-y, and everything is in perfect shape. It's lady dressing to a tee. There's even a good selection of vintage lingerie, if you can stomach that sort of thing.

Leather sandals are a sometimes difficult thing to get right: too minimal and they're uncomfortable, too supportive and you're Mother Earth, so it's good to know about **Jutta Neumann**, where you can sort this balance out by designing a pair of your own.

One of the things that well-dressed women pride themselves on is everything being sorted underneath, which is why **Orchard Corset Discount Center** is such a culty hit. It's a cramped little bra shop on Orchard Street manned by a mother/son team of Orthodox Jews. Junior sizes you (and occasionally feels you up), tells you what you need, and then Mom hurries you behind a shabby little curtain where she pushes and prods you into a (decidedly plain) perfectly fitted bra. Generations of New York women absolutely swear by Orchard Corset. And it's such a good story once you're done.

EAST VILLAGE

Shopping in the East Village is a New York rite of style-passage. It's where one goes to get pierced, to get a tattoo, or just to find some thoroughly inappropriate boots.

Sofia Hedstrom (see pages 74–75), on Fourth Ave. between 8th and 9th Sts.

What age you are when you go through your East Village thing depends on a complicated ratio of where you grew up to how religious your parents were to how you feel about Joe Strummer from the Clash.

We've met some great Look Book subjects in the East Village, like Sofia Hedstrom in her minty green kneesocks, and Al the Cowboy, combing the aisles of Kmart. It's the kind of place where the way to stand out is by wearing khakis from the Gap.

Trash & Vaudeville is ground zero for the patent-leather thigh-high boots and fishnet stockings that ultimately look better ripped. They also stock a full range of unflattering lipsticks. It's for goths, or temporary goths, or for Halloween.

Many a fashion editor or model can be found sheepishly unloading her freebies at the resale shop **Tokyo Joe**, where they are resold by a strict and gruff Japanese staff. There are good things to be found as well as endless racks of things that look like they might give you a rash.

Gabay's is a mysterious discount store that sells extremely high-end stuff extremely cheaply. They do a terrible job of X-ing out, with a Sharpie, the merchandise's origin

WHERE TO SHOP

1. **Trash & Vaudeville**
   4 St. Marks Place at Third Ave.
   212-982-3590

2. **Tokyo Joe**
   334 E. 11th St. nr. Second Ave.
   212-473-0724

3. **Gabay's**
   225 First Ave. nr. 13th St.
   212-529-4036

4. **Cobblestones**
   314 E. 9th St. nr. Second Ave.
   212-673-5372

5. **Blue**
   137 Avenue A nr. 9th St.
   212-228-7744

6. **Amarcord**
   84 E. 7th St. nr. First Ave.
   212-614-7133
   amarcordvintagefashion.com

7. **Momo Falana**
   43 Avenue A nr. 3rd St.
   212-979-9595
   momofalana.com

8. **Alpana Bawa**
   70 E. 1st St. nr. First Ave.
   212-254-1249
   alpanabawa.com

9. **Anna**
   150 E. 3rd St. nr. Avenue A
   212-358-0195
   annanyc.com

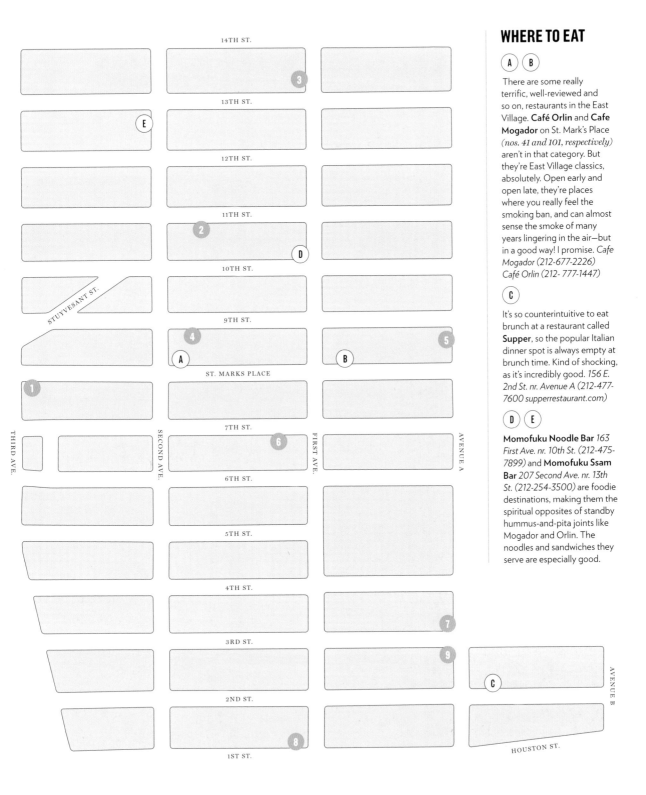

WHERE TO EAT

(A) (B)

There are some really terrific, well-reviewed and so on, restaurants in the East Village. **Café Orlin** and **Cafe Mogador** on St. Mark's Place *(nos. 41 and 101, respectively)* aren't in that category. But they're East Village classics, absolutely. Open early and open late, they're places where you really feel the smoking ban, and can almost sense the smoke of many years lingering in the air—but in a good way! I promise. *Cafe Mogador (212-677-2226) Café Orlin (212- 777-1447)*

(C)

It's so counterintuitive to eat brunch at a restaurant called **Supper**, so the popular Italian dinner spot is always empty at brunch time. Kind of shocking, as it's incredibly good. *156 E. 2nd St. nr. Avenue A (212-477-7600 supperrestaurant.com)*

(D) (E)

Momofuku Noodle Bar *163 First Ave. nr. 10th St. (212-475-7899)* and **Momofuku Ssam Bar** *207 Second Ave. nr. 13th St. (212-254-3500)* are foodie destinations, making them the spiritual opposites of standby hummus-and-pita joints like Mogador and Orlin. The noodles and sandwiches they serve are especially good.

(Bergdorf Goodman) and original price (exorbitant). Why Bergdorf's dumps its off-season, unsold merchandise here is a mystery I'm not terribly interested in solving, but they do, and it explains the $1,800 handbags on the shoulders of many savvy neighborhood girls.

Cobblestones is a strange, cramped vintage shop where most of the merchandise seems to be from the fifties. I can't shop here without getting the giggles, as the proprietor likes to be-bop along to the jazz records when you least expect it. Be prepared.

Brides who consider themselves "not very bride" (you know the type, they have male "bridesmaids," write their own vows, and serve vegan cupcakes for dessert) get their dresses made at **Blue**. They are actually quite chic dresses, not terribly experimental, but there is something wonderful about needing to dry-clean the cigarette ash out of your dress before wearing it. Also: lots of un-white dresses, for bridesmaids or just for friends who like to dress up.

Amarcord is yet another vintage shop—the neighborhood is lousy with them!—but all of the stuff at Amarcord comes from Italy.

People who refuse to admit that the seventies are over find bliss at **Momo Falana**, in tie-dyed muumuus and sundresses. It's for a Stevie Nicks-Janis Joplin aspirant, but since haute hippie is so frequently in high fashion, the dresses here always pop up in fashion magazines' "bohemia" spreads.

Alpana Bawa is for people who like—as in really, really, really like—color. Rich, saturated, drunk-on-color color; color fantastic enough for a Mira Nair set.

Anna is one of those lovely East Village shops that makes you grateful not to live in a place where your only option is shopping in a mall. The designer is Kathy Kemp, and she's usually at the store, encouraging clients to layer a few skirts on at a time. The quality isn't tremendous, but the clothes are the types of things you don't see everywhere, and you can, authentically, answer "just some little shop in the East Village" if anyone asks you where your dress is from.

WEST VILLAGE

It's hard to keep up with the shopping scene in the West Village.

Brian Sullivan, and his daughter, Saoirse (see pages 88–89), photographed on the corner of Bleecker and 11th Sts.

Every time I walk down Bleecker Street, another oddball laundromat/bookshop/cheapyy antiques shop has been converted to something glossy, like Ralph Lauren, Cynthia Rowley, or the dread fashion virus that is Intermix. As our cover girl, Kay Goldberg, put it when the Look Book met her on the corner of Bleecker and West 11th Streets as she made her way home from school: "It seems more like a place to be than a place where you are."

No matter what shops open on Bleecker Street, it will remain Avenue Marc Jacobs. There's **Marc by Marc Jacobs** for men (*403 Bleecker*) and women (*405 Bleecker*), and a separate accessories shop (*385 Bleecker*) selling pieces from the grown-up, super-expensive Marc Jacobs Collection. What makes these Marc Jacobs stores better than other Marc Jacobs stores is that they are the designer's home base. Yes, they sell mounds of Marc merch—gobs of it, in fact. But there are always nice surprises, too, like a window full of Francine Prose's latest novel, Hillary Clinton T-shirts, and $35 rubber wellies if it happens to be raining a lot.

When **Castor & Pollux** moved from Brooklyn to West 10th Street, it brought with it a lovely, indy spirit. It's not a chain or some mega-brand's "cool" outpost. I love the store's big plate-glass picture windows, and that it's full of great clothes by designers like Phillip Lim, Mint, and Sonia Rykiel. Sometimes the clothes at Castor & Pollux seem like the clothes that girls wear to impress other girls (as opposed to, say, clothes that girls wear to impress boys, or bosses, or future mothers-in-law), which is to say that they are quite often beautiful, quite regularly cool, but not always sexy or tidy.

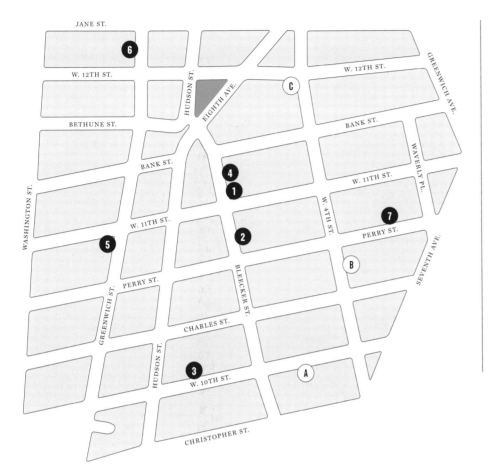

WHERE TO EAT

Don't wait at Magnolia, but do wait at **Westville**; it's worth it. All sorts of green-market vegetables, fantastic burgers, and a good, neighborhood vibe. *210 W. 10th St. nr. Bleecker St. (212-741-7971)*

Sant Ambroeus is expensive, yes, but very, very chic. Fashion people like to eat here, drink here, gossip here. So if you're having a shopping sort of day, why not? *259 W. 4th St. at Perry St. (212-604-9254 antambroeus.com)*

Cafe Cluny is another great fashion-spotting restaurant. I like to sit by the windows, for double the people watching. *284 W. 12th St. at W. 4th St. (212-255-6900)*

As T-shirt technology marches on towards some apex of softness, **James Perse** somehow remains ahead of the game. These shirts are unbelievably soft. They feel, from the first time you pick them up, like you've owned them for years, which is probably some sinister marketing plot, but it works. You'll want a whole batch of them and to wear nothing else. But then you'd have to move to Los Angeles.

At a moment when all groovy men's stores seem compelled to get themselves up like Victorian hunting lodges, **Oliver Spencer** may look like just another faux-woodsman's enclave. (Must every shop have antlers and a terrarium? Yes, it seems, if straight men are expected to participate in Fashion with a capital F.) But the clothes are good and solid: fashionable, but still masculine, which can be a tricky balance.

Obvious pretensions aside—no sign, for starters—**Maison Martin Margiela** is a great store. Persevere! Margiela clothes are classic, with subtle, clever twists. Wearing Margiela is like being part of a secret fashion cult, as your Margiela this or that will always be recognized as such by a certain cognoscenti! Men's and women's clothes, and, occasionally, vintage shoes.

Geminola is an outrageously charming splinter of a store on an otherwise shopping-free stretch of Perry Street. It's filled with vintage slips and lace and things all dyed fantastic, rich colors in a handmade sort of way, as if they'd been soaked in Rit dye and stirred by the grooviest camp counselor at your nature camp, circa 1971. Prepare yourself, however, for the prices. They're kind of insane. This is the West Village, where, unless they've got rent control, hippies are haute.

DESTINATION

MEATPACKING

Wedged between the West Village and Chelsea, the Meatpacking District has become terribly trendy.

Neville Wakefield (see pages 208–209), spotted on Ninth Ave. and 13th St.

The good news is that it doesn't smell so much like blood anymore. The bad news is the crowds—particularly at night. We tried to shoot one early fall evening across the street from the Gansevoort Hotel, and it was a total disappointment. There were drunk frat boys jumping on the set (every time we shoot, at least one guy jumps onto the set and announces that he's ready for his close-up with utter conviction that he's the first guy to ever make this joke. In the Meatpacking District on a Thursday night, there were dozens.) But the bigger problem for Look Book purposes was that everyone was dressed alike. That said, there's some decent shopping if you pick carefully.

The Meatpacking District during the day, however, is something else entirely. It's positively packed with places to shop.

Jeffrey was the first fancy shop on the strip of 14th Street, and, given its geographical bravery, its selection has always been surprisingly tame. Glamorous labels, yes, but conservative buys. The real reason to shop Jeffrey is for the incredible shoe department. Endless designers and a real sensitivity to sizes (if they don't have it, they'll try to find it and they won't make you feel a yeti in the process) make it quite possibly the best place to buy expensive shoes in the city.

Tenthousandthings is a New York institution: elegant jewelry that announces itself quietly, but certainly announces itself. The charm necklaces are a real status symbol among a certain type of fashion editor (the type who acts confused by Botox), who tend to collect and layer them. It's also a real hangout for the West Village celebrity, a breed far more suspicious of "bling" than her West Coast counterpart: e.g. Julianne Moore, Maggie Gyllenhaal.

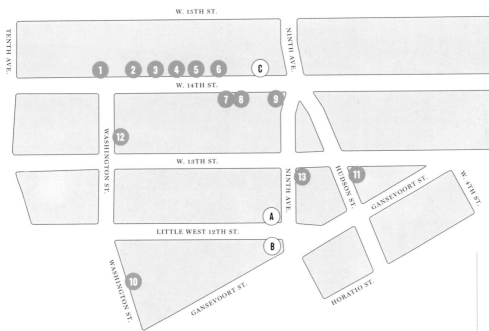

Stella McCartney, Alexander McQueen, La Perla, Carlos Miele, Yigal Azrouel. There are so many shiny designer shops on this block, and it always seems like they're empty. McCartney and McQueen are probably best for browsing, as they're extremely expensive, and everything they sell can be found in a big department store as well. McCartney shoes, though, are one major exception. If you're a fashion vegan, it's a run-don't-walk situation, as McCartney shoes are chic and bold, and never have even a touch of leather on them anywhere. McQueen clothes are best for statement-making, and Azrouel's are best for layering. Carlos Miele is kind of like a Brazilian Cavalli, and La Perla is La Perla—dirty underpants, of the silkiest variety. (Catriona MacKechnie across the street has loads of lingerie as well, by a bunch of different labels.)

This is a great neighborhood for buying jeans; where else, after all, can you find two custom denim shops within spitting distance: An Earnest Cut & Sew and Jean Shop. Both customize your jeans, which is different from having them made from scratch, which is to say, you can choose a number of variables (washes, sizes, styles) and put them all together.

Catherine Malandrino doesn't change drastically from season to season: She makes dresses with nipped waists and slouchy, off-the-shoulder sweaters. Boys find their girlfriends sexy in Catherine Malandrino dresses, which is perhaps why so many pop up at summer weddings and junior committee cocktail parties. There's inevitably a lot of lacy white in a Malandrino collection, and there is frequently a beret. Most thrilling, however, is her new collaboration with Repetto, a French brand of dance shoes.

Dernier Cri is dedicated to finding young designers with weird names and weird visions and selling their stuff. Which means it can be hit or miss in there: Sometimes that zip-up-denim-whatsit is a splendid surprise, other times less so. Curiously, it's right next to the least original of New York chains, Scoop. Scoop is where to go if you like your hair straight, your boots Ugg, and your sweats Juicy.

Henry Beguelin is a leather shop, though not a leather shop the way there used to be leather shops around here. It's a soft, tooled leather shop, with knapsacks, baby slings, and handmade-ish shoes that have charmingly irregular soles and laces.

WHERE TO EAT

(A)

Pastis is the neighborhood gold standard. On weekend nights, it gets clogged up with tourists in all of their "downtown" finery. Breakfast and lunch tend to be a bit mellower, though there can be a major wait. Expect glorious parading of status accessories. *9 Ninth Ave. at Little W. 12th St. (212-929-4844 pastisny.com)*

(B)

Paradou is across the street and far mellower. Incredible crêpes, tamer crowd, and that sort of "Frenchness" that makes you think it's perfectly all right to drink during the day. *8 Little W. 12th St. nr. Ninth Ave. (212.463.8345 paradounyc.com)*

(C)

When shopping, pie for lunch at **The Little Pie Company** strikes me as perfectly reasonable. Sour cream apple walnut, in particular. *407 W. 14th St. nr. Ninth Ave. (212-414-2324 littlepiecompany.com)*

CHELSEA

Chelsea is undoubtedly a great place to shop if you're in the market for assless chaps or handcuffs. But it can also be quite chic.

McCloud Zicmuse (see pages 146–147), on the corner of Ninth Ave. and 25th St.

There are several distinct zones in Chelsea: There's the South-Beach-in-Manhattan stretch of Eighth Avenue, all bright colors and assless chaps. Farther west it's Soho-in-the-eighties: stark galleries and just a few, avant garde boutiques. That's where we found McCloud Zicmuse gallery hopping on a crowded Thursday night.

One can't describe shopping in Chelsea without shouting out at least a few places to find a nice leather vest-and-chaps set. **Camouflage**, **Purple Passion**, and (need we even say it?) **Arcadia** fill these, and other dark, domination-y, needs. They're also handy for punks.

Balenciaga and **Comme des Garçons** are two of the most intimidating shops in the city. For one thing, they sell scary fashion:

That is, fashion that you might not "get" right away because it is extreme and expensive, and these shops always have the kind of salespeople who can smell your Gap khakis halfway down the block. They feel important architecturally, as if to announce that these are not mere retail stores, they are Important Design Sites. And they are not in Soho, or on Madison Avenue, as if their location amongst important art galleries places their clothes closer to art than to fashion. But! As with any store, it's not really worth being intimidated. It's a store. It exists to sell you things, or to allow you to gaze at really impressive feats of design. Comme des Garçons also happens to have the best wallets, and they're not even 200 bucks. And if you're in the mood to drop high four figures

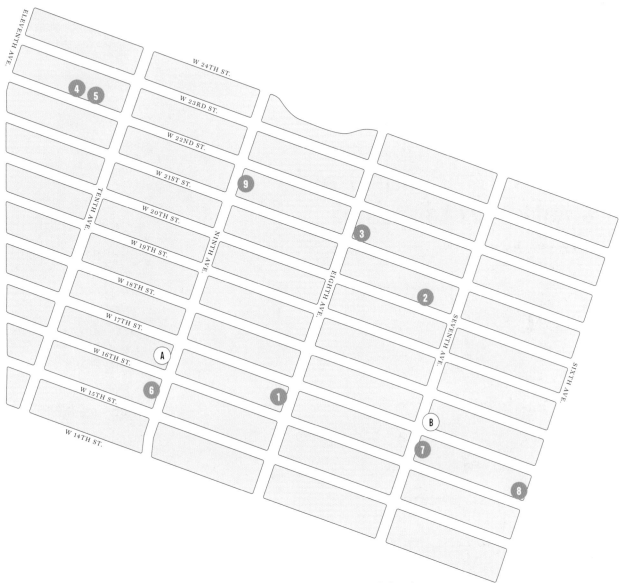

on something, the edition pieces at Balenciaga, which are re-issues of the house's vintage designs, haven't gone out of style yet, and are unlikely to.

202/Nicole Farhi always makes me feel very American, because it is just so English and there is a café inside where you can order one of those thoroughly greasy and fat-making breakfasts. It feels like a country house, and the clothes are something you'd wear should you be invited on a country weekend by someone English and glamorously bohemian.

Loehmann's is Loehmann's, and many a New York girl of my generation came to terms with body image by stripping bare before several generations of her relatives in a Loehmann's group dressing room. I certainly did. Loehmann's isn't for the faint of heart, and there's always the sense that the best discount stuff lands at Century 21, and that Loehmann's is for the grandmas. But for the tough, it's always worth a scour.

Dave's New York sells work clothes— like Carhart pants and insulated hoodie sweatshirts. It's what the guys who like Steven Alan and Freemans add to their wardrobes in order to have some authentic masculinity in there with all calculated stuff.

Everything at **parke & ronen** is cut on the narrow side. Whenever I walk past the shop, I swear I can smell the cologne and see the hair gel on the mannequins. I can also always picture these clothes hanging neatly in someone's locker at the David Barton gym.

WHERE TO EAT

(A)

202 is always nice, for the reasons mentioned at left, and the fresh-squeezed juice is good and pulpy. *75 Ninth Ave. nr. 16th St. (646-638-1173)*

(B)

Cafeteria is full of gorgeous waiters and low-carb lunches. *115 Seventh Ave. nr. 17th St. (212-414-1717)*

UNION SQUARE

Union Square has proven fantastically ripe for Look Book scouting.

Mica DeJesus (see pages 18–19), spotted at Union Square West and E. 15th St.

Union Square is where we met John Waters on his way to the 6 train—when approached, he said, "Oh, I love the Look Book, but it typically features people who are quite unknown"—and Crystal Boria on a break from nursing school. The mornings are full of smart-looking organic yuppies buying apples and yams, and in the afternoons there are masses of kids skateboarding, protesting, and flirting.

The shopping in and just around Union Square tends toward large chain shops. So shooting here allows us to see the ways that those skateboarding, protesting, flirting kids have put these seemingly banal elements together to create something totally original.

Union Square is anchored by a several-floors-deep behemoth housing the stores **Forever 21, DSW,** and **Filene's Basement**. It's not a particularly pleasant shopping experience—lights are bright and fluorescent, for one thing—but it's fantastic for on-trend bargains. You do have to be about 21 years old to look good in most of them, but never mind. At **Forever 21,** the prices are genuinely low, shockingly so sometimes. **DSW** really varies: Every once in a while there will be a pair of Marc by Marc Jacobs d'Orsay pumps.

The **Diesel** shop can sometimes feel a bit dated: Diesel was the premium denim brand before hairstylists and pop tarts and former *Real World* cast members all had premium denim brands of their own. But it is what it is; the music is loud, the staff is eager, helpful, and loaded up on hair product.

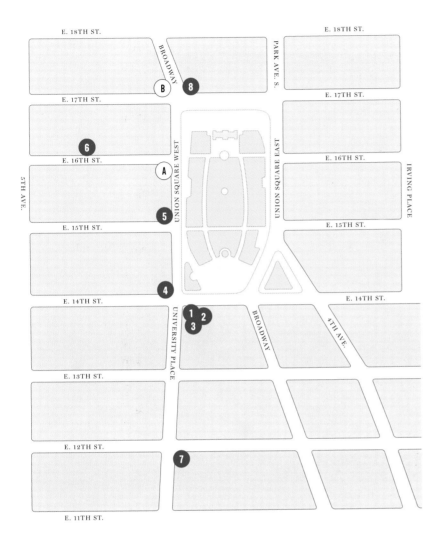

E. 18TH ST. — E. 18TH ST.

BROADWAY

PARK AVE. S.

B 8

E. 17TH ST. — E. 17TH ST.

UNION SQUARE WEST

UNION SQUARE EAST

IRVING PLACE

6

A

E. 16TH ST. — E. 16TH ST.

5TH AVE.

5

E. 15TH ST. — E. 15TH ST.

4

E. 14TH ST. — E. 14TH ST.

UNIVERSITY PLACE

1 2
3

BROADWAY

4TH AVE.

E. 13TH ST.

E. 12TH ST.

7

E. 11TH ST.

WHERE TO EAT

The Coffee Shop is one of those New York institution-type places where there are endless rumors regarding the attractiveness of the waitstaff (They're all models! That type of thing) and the seating policy is allegedly based, again, on attractiveness. In the summer, the outdoor tables on the Union Square side are prime. *29 Union Sq. West at 16th St. (212-243-7969)*

The first time I went to **Tisserie**, I thought it seemed like the type of place you'd find in a really lovely European train station. But it's better than that—quite delicious, really—for pastries and coffee and sandwiches on baguettes. *857 Broadway at 17th St. (212-463-0850)*

American Eagle Outfitters is, perhaps, a more democratic Abercrombie & Fitch—tank tops for layering, endless iterations on a cargo pant. If you're young, you can buy all of your clothes here. If you're not, you probably can't, but you can buy weekend-y sweatshirts and the like.

Agnès B. is off Union Square on 16th Street, and thank God for it, or you'd wander Union Square thinking that anyone older than 25 is meant to go naked. The clothes always walk that dowdy/French line that makes me think it's all in the attitude. So if you have the right (French) attitude, go nuts. The button-down shirts and soft cotton cardigans make me feel like the star of an Eric Roehmer movie.

Rugby is Ralph Lauren's answer to the Abercrombie & Fitch market. The specialty is, unsurprisingly, rugby shirts, which they'll doctor up for you with all sorts of patches and so on. The clothes are preppy, like much of Ralph Lauren, but here they are cheaper, in order to be affordable to the NYU students in and around the shop.

David Z, on the northern side of Union Square, is hectic and loud, but it's where one gets the staples of New York footwear: Ugg boots, Converse, and Vans. These are not fancy shoes; rather, they are the shoes people actually wear in order to survive in a walking city, while keeping the beauties in a bag.

MADISON/FIFTH AVES.

Even someone who's never set foot on the island of Manhattan could probably tell you that Madison Avenue is where to go shopping. And they wouldn't be wrong...

The corner of Madison and 61st Street, just opposite Barneys, is probably where we've shot more Look Books than any other single corner in town. We met Robin Chandler Duke there on her way to her River House apartment from delivering a lecture at the Pierre. We met the George family there on a Saturday afternoon shopping trip, and also Thelma Schnitzer, the first-ever Look Book subject.

The retail madness starts in the high 50s and stretches for 30 or so blocks north: retail madness! Every fabulous brand has a fabulous shop that probably doesn't earn loads of money but does announce that said brand is, in fact, fabulous.

So where to begin? Really, it's about the stroll and the window shopping and the admiring of the fancy people— the New Yorkers and the smooth European tourists with their perfect loafers and tans. I won't bother describing the niceness of the Chloe, or Valentino, or Oscar de la Renta boutiques (it's not too difficult to imagine), but here are a few highlights:

Barneys New York may well be the best store in the world. It starts with the ground floor bonanza of jewelry and bags and perfect scarves and shawls, and then there are seven more floors of fantastic. What makes Barneys so good is the selection: Yes, you can find

WHERE TO SHOP

1. **Bergdorf Goodman**
754 Fifth Ave. bet. 57th and 58th Sts.
212-753-7300
bergdorfgoodman.com

2. **Barneys**
660 Madison Ave. nr. 61st St.
212-826-8900
barneys.com

3. **Sonia Rykiel**
849 Madison Ave. nr. 70th St.
212-396-3060
soniarykiel.com

4. **45rpm**
17 E. 71st St. bet. Fifth and Madison Aves.
212-737-5545
rby45rpm.com

5. **Ralph Lauren**
867 Madison Ave. bet. 71st and 72nd Sts.
212-434-8000
polo.com

6. **Calypso**
935 Madison Ave. at 74th
212-535-4100
calypso-celle.com

7. **Christian Louboutin**
941 Madison Ave. nr. 74th St.
212-396-1884
christianlouboutin.fr

8. **Vera Wang**
991 Madison Ave. nr. 77th St.
212-628-3400
verawang.com

9. **Peress Lingerie**
1006 Madison at 78th St.
212-861-6336

10. **Vilebrequin**
1070 Madison Ave., at E. 81st St.
212-650-0353

11. **Tender Buttons**
143 62nd St. at Lexington Ave. (off the map)
212-758-7004

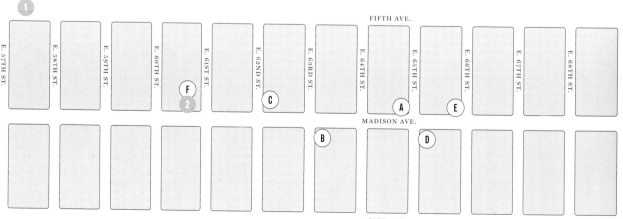

Oleg Cassini (see pages 32–33), spotted on the corner of Madison Ave. and 61st St.

(see pages 32–33)

WHERE TO EAT

A

Try the cafés of Madison in the 60s. There are plenty of them with nice sidewalk seating and dependable steak frites on the menu. **La Goulue** *746 Madison Ave., between 64th and 65th Sts. (212-988-8169)* is a favorite among the shoppers—during winter, it's best avoided by PETA members.

B **C** **D** **E**

Le Bilboquet *25 E. 63rd St. nr. Madison Ave. (212-751-3036)* is popular with people who don't find it embarrassing to refer to themselves, casually, as Eurotrash, and **Amaranth** *21 E. 62nd St. (212-980-6700)*, **Ferrier** *29 E. 65th St. (212-772-9000)*, and **Fredericks Madison** *768 Madison Ave. bet. 65th and 66th Sts. (212-737-7300)* are similarly packed with people who dry-clean their jeans.

F

Fred's at Barneys can be a people-watching riot, with everyone appearing fabulously shellacked and on-trend, and there's always the occasional pop star with her mom. They're very used to nutty diet requests at Fred's, and they, perversely I've always thought, also serve the most delicious French fries. *660 Madison Ave. at 60th St. (212-833-2200)*

---

all things fancy, but you can also find brands you probably can't find in other places, like striped socks from Japan, and the Nepali pashmina of exactly the right weight. Barneys has personality and a sense of humor. The first jewelry case inside the door is full of crystals wrapped in thick gold wire and if you come on the right afternoon, you'll find the designer in all white, and she'd be delighted to discuss your chakra.

Peress Lingerie is a wonderfully old-fashioned lingerie shop, where you're seldom allowed to handle the merch—you discuss your needs with the old couple who run the place, and they expertly sort through endless stacks

of Perspex boxes marked with labels like "Hanro lace trim tank." It's not a chain, it's not too fancy, it's a complete throwback, and I hope it lasts forever.

There are so many **Calypso** stores all over the city, but the Calypso megastore here deserves special mention because it's Calypso HQ: five stories of all things Calypso.

It's not on Madison Avenue, but if you don't mind a short walk east, investigate **Tender Buttons**, which sells only buttons. It's perfect.

The **Christian Louboutin** shop feels exactly as an expensive shoe shop should: luxurious. At the risk of

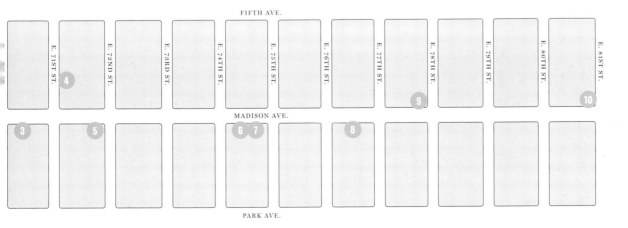

FIFTH AVE.

E. 71ST ST. | E. 72ND ST. | E. 73RD ST. | E. 74TH ST. | E. 75TH ST. | E. 76TH ST. | E. 77TH ST. | E. 78TH ST. | E. 79TH ST. | E. 80TH ST. | E. 81ST ST.

MADISON AVE.

PARK AVE.

Lisa Falcone (see pages 218–219), on the corner of Madison Ave. and 61st St.

using a cliché, it feels like a jewel box, each pair of shoes a gem. Which they should be, at $500 and up.

Every fashionable man seems to have acquired, in the last four or five years, a pair of **Vilebrequin** swimming trunks, which means that fancy beaches in St. Barths and the Hamptons are positively loaded with them. I think this is because Vilebrequin filled a genuine need in the market for appropriately modest, discreet shapes and enough color and pattern to keep men from feeling dull.

The **Ralph Lauren** mansion is always worth a visit, mostly because here you are, smack in the middle of the Upper East Side, and why wouldn't you drop by? It's a masterpiece of display and affectation, a true mark of brilliance in the history of American retail, a reminder of this country's deep fetishization of the WASP. It sometimes feels more museum than shop, but it's a definite reminder of how style can be transcendent.

45rpm is a co-ed line of simple Japanese clothing made from the nicest, richest,

and most organic of fibers. T-shirts all rolled up feel somehow virtuous to wear: the fashion equivalent of delicious, pure sashimi or miso soup.

I mention **Vera Wang** not for the legendary wedding dresses, but for the ready-to-wear clothes, which too many people forget about. They're the product of years spent yearning for color and freedom, and they're exquisite.

Bergdorf Goodman is an entire block of delight—a shop for the chic-est people in town. Almost every brilliant label has a well-lit, soft little pod devoted to it, and the shoe department is probably the best on Earth. On the fifth floor there's a magical selection of jeans and groovier designers you didn't know you could find so close to Central Park.

Sonia Rykiel has never made the splash here that she does in Paris, where her red hair is a legendary sight during lunch at the Café Flore. But the clothes are every bit as foxy here as they are there, and the handbags every bit as iconic.

CARROLL GARDENS BOERUM HILL COBBLE HILL

Far yuppier than Williamsburg, this neighborhood is fast turning into an affordable version of the West Village, with double stroller jams aplenty.

Also, thanks to the lower rents, several of our favorite multi-mark boutiques are here.

Bird is run by a former Steven Alan buyer, and it's full of labels that are hard to find on the other side of the river, like Tsumori Chisato and Vanessa Bruno, Vena Cava, Isabel Marant— and some that are easier to find, such as A.P.C., Mayle, and 3.1 Phillip Lim. I would ride the F train just to shop here, because it's fashion-y but not obvious.

Butter carries fashion-ambitious labels like Dries Van Noten and Zero Maria Cornejo, as well as soft Clu T-shirts and Marni shoes. It's not excessively feminine; it's more urban-feminine, which is to say that dark colors often dominate, and the pervasive spirit is that women who shop here know how to dress themselves without much fawning.

Frida's Closet is an entire shop devoted to emulating and drawing inspiration from the spirit of Frida Kahlo. Most people won't find anything here, but thank God a shop based on so nutty a premise can still exist somewhere in New York.

With so many Manhattan office-types riding the F train, it only makes sense that **Diane T** should follow. Full of designer jeans and Rebecca Taylor dresses, it's kind of one-stop shopping for, say, an ad exec or a lawyer on the weekend.

For certain people, a move across the East River is a thing of huge pride: they like to gloat about the extra space, extra sky, leafy views and "community." These people like **Brooklyn Industries** hoodies. It's now a whole brand, with a chicken-or-the-egg tendency to match exactly what everyone's wearing at the Bergen Street station.

WHERE TO SHOP

1 Bird
220 Smith St. nr. Butler St.
718-797-3774
shopbird.com

2 Butter
389 Atlantic Ave. bet. Hoyt and Bond Sts.
718-260-9033

3 Frida's Closet
296 Smith St. nr. Union St.
718-855-0311
fridascloset.com

4 Diane T
174 Court St. nr. Bergen St.
718-923-5777

5 Brooklyn Industries
100 Smith St. nr. Atlantic Ave.
718-596-3986
brooklynindustries.com

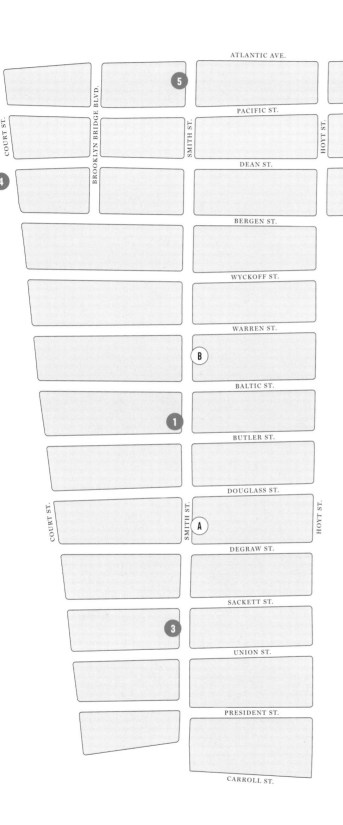

ATLANTIC AVE.

PACIFIC ST.

DEAN ST.

BERGEN ST.

WYCKOFF ST.

WARREN ST.

BALTIC ST.

BUTLER ST.

DOUGLASS ST.

DEGRAW ST.

SACKETT ST.

UNION ST.

PRESIDENT ST.

CARROLL ST.

COURT ST.

BROOKLYN BRIDGE BLVD.

SMITH ST.

HOYT ST.

BOND ST.

COURT ST.

SMITH ST.

HOYT ST.

WHERE TO EAT

Patois is cozy and French— in the wintertime there's a fireplace and in the summer the outdoor garden is lovely. Brunch is a bargain at $12, but there's usually a wait. Pop into Bird across the street. *255 Smith St. nr. DeGraw St. (718-855-1535)*

Robin des Bois is heavy on the kitsch where decor is concerned: don't even consider eating here if you consider yourself a minimalist. You'll go nuts. *195 Smith St. nr. Warren St. (718-596-1609)*

Kyle Mingo (see pages 100–101), photographed at Fulton Street Mall.

WILLIAMSBURG

As Brooklyn gentrifies, the shopping follows.

Bobby Vita (see pages 188–189), spotted at Bedford Ave. and N. 7th St.

Williamsburg can be alarmingly hip. Everyone seems to take credit for ironic T-shirts, bedhead, and electroclash. Some of our subjects, like Janicza Bravo, find it inspirational, while Bobby Vita, whom we met on North 6th Street, seems unaware that the neighborhood has changed at all.

Shopping in Williamsburg ranges, like the neighborhood itself, from DIY-ish to trendy and expensive.

It's a fantastic place to find style on the streets, because everyone is making an effort to look original, unique, clever, creative, something. There are, naturally, hits and misses, but it's one of the city's best style labs.

Triple Five Soul is classic Brooklyn B-boy gear, which, at press time, hasn't gone out of style and, we're hoping, won't anytime soon.

Otte is not unlike Scoop, with its mix of trendy, upscale brands; it just happens to be in Williamsburg, so it's a bit groovier. These are definitely clothes for people living in the new luxury

condos, not the old loft conversions that don't get heat on the weekends.

Ylli and **Jumelle**: both multi-mark, higher-end boutiques that reinforce the image of Williamsburg as dense with "trustafarians." Ylli is less fancy, more groovy. It's more what you'd wear as a grad student than what you'd wear as, say, a gallery assistant, which is who, you get the impression, shops at Jumelle.

Beacon's Closet gets mentioned during Look Book interviews more than any other single shop. Perhaps we gravitate towards vintage shoppers, but perhaps its because it's a fantastic toolshop for assembling unique looks. It's vintage, which means it's all one of a kind, or is at this point anyway, and it's well edited and curated by savvy-eyed Williamsburgers.

The cool little sister to a Park Slope shop of the same name, **Oak** plays on Williamsburg's stark, industrial vibe, with concrete floors and white walls These are clothes for people who long to live in Antwerp, vacation in Iceland, and keep Björk on the heavy rotation.

WHERE TO SHOP

1 **Triple Five Soul**
145 Bedford Ave. at N. 9th St.
718-599-597
triple5soul.com

2 **Otte**
132 N. 5th St. nr. Bedford Ave.
718-302-3007

3 **Ylli**
482 Driggs Ave. at N. 10th St.
718-302-3555
yllibklyn.com

4 **Jumelle**
148 Bedford Ave. nr. N. 9th St.
718-388-9525
shopjumelle.com

5 **Beacon's Closet**
88 N. 11th St. nr. Wythe Ave.
718-486-0816
beaconscloset.com

6 **Oak**
208 N. 8th St. bet. Driggs Ave. and Roebling St.
718-782-0521
oaknyc.com

WHERE TO EAT

A

If you don't mind a little walk from the shop-dense area of Williamsburg by the Bedford Avenue L stop, head down Bedford toward Broadway. First you'll pass **Bonita**, *338 Bedford Ave. between S. 2nd and S. 3rd Sts. (718-384-9500)* a sort of raucous/fabulous Mexican place where salty chips and margaritas make everything more flattering.

B

Once you get to Broadway, turn left for **Dressler**, *149 Broadway between Driggs and Bedford Aves. (718-384-6343),* with its fabulous wrought-iron details and delicious bar food.

C **D**

Turn right for **Diner**, *85 Broadway at Berry St. (718-486-3077)* and **Marlow & Sons**, *81 Broadway between Berry St. and Wythe Ave. (718-384-1441).* Deceptive in their simplicity, they're considered by many of the bedhead set to be the coolest restaurants in the city. Diner is green-market fresh, while Marlow and Sons is a little grocery with a sandwich shop in back. Eat up, yes, but watch the outfits for sure.

N. 12TH ST.
N. 11TH ST.
N. 10TH ST.
N. 9TH ST.
N. 8TH ST.
N. 7TH ST.
N. 6TH ST.
N. 5TH ST.
N. 4TH ST.
N. 3RD ST.
METROPOLITAN AVE.
N. 1ST ST.
GRAND ST.
S. 1ST ST.
S. 2ND ST.
S. 3RD ST.
S. 4TH ST.
S. 5TH ST.
S. 6TH ST.
S. 8TH ST.
S. 9TH ST.

KENT AVE.
WYTHE AVE.
BERRY ST.
BEDFORD AVE.
DRIGGS AVE.
ROEBLING ST.
ROEBLING AVE.

WILLIAMSBURG BRIDGE

BROADWAY

ACKNOWLEDGMENTS

—

Thank you to Adam Moss, our editor-in-chief, for his great understanding that the most interesting people in New York are not always famous.

The Look Book lives in the Strategist, where many fantastic editors have been involved. Amy Goldwasser developed the entire section before leaving it in the capable hands of Ben Williams, Janet Ozzard, and Jonathan Paul.

Thanks also to Emily Nussbaum, who edited the parts of this book not previously published.

The *New York* magazine photo department, led by Jody Quon, deserves a tremendous amount of credit for dealing with the various bureaucracies associated with street photography, and for always choosing the perfect shots. Extra thanks specifically to Leana Alagia.

The design of the column and, largely, of this book is thanks to the splendid eyes of Luke Hayman, Chris Dixon, John Sheppard, and Randy Minor.

Ann Clarke was unbelievably patient and kind in bringing this book's many moving parts together. Serena Torrey acted as a godmother to this book from the beginning, and it wouldn't exist without her dedication.

Our agent, David McCormick, went from Look Book fan to Look Book champion, and we are grateful. Holly Rothman and Jessi Rymill patiently dealt with the many cooks this book brought to the kitchen. Special thanks to Molly Logan for all of her support.

Tremendous gratitude goes to Jill Weiskopf, Wren Abbot, and Nick Hofstadter for tracking down every single Look Booker and securing permissions, and to Kit Taylor, Eric Bergner, Lisa Goren, and Mike Malone.

Photo Assistants Spencer Heyfron, Kevin Trageser, Andrew Sutherland, Dominic Nietz, Isa Wipfli, Nick D'Emilio, and Jeremy Williams have stayed in fantastic humor during terrible weather, bomb threats, traffic jams, and Richard Lee has kept Jake's studio running smoothly.

Thank you to David Hazan, Richard Foulser, Phil South, Alec Friedman, and Becci Manson at Picturehouse for all their hard work and dedication in making sure the images look so fantastic and being so generous their time.

Special thanks also to Lisa Davis, Harriet and Ava Chessum, Jim, Dale, Josh, and Mike Larocca, and to Will Frears.

Melcher Media would like to thank David E. Brown, Daniel Del Valle, Mark Miller, Lauren Nathan, Lia Ronnen, Tim Soter, Lindsey Stanberry, Alex Tart, Carl Williamson, Betty Wong, and Megan Worman.